SWIFT'S IRISH PAMPHLETS
AN INTRODUCTORY SELECTION

Ulster Editions and Monographs
General Editors
Robert Welch
John McVeagh

ULSTER EDITIONS AND MONOGRAPHS SERIES
(ISSN 0954–3392)

SWIFT'S IRISH PAMPHLETS

An Introductory Selection

Edited by
Joseph McMinn

Ulster Editions and Monographs 2

COLIN SMYTHE
Gerrards Cross, 1991

First published in 1991 in Great Britain by Colin Smythe Limited,
Gerrards Cross, Buckinghamshire

British Library Cataloguing in Publication Data

Swift, Jonathan, *1667–1745*
Swift's Irish pamphlets : an
introductory selection. — (Ulster editions and
monographs; ISSN 09543392, 2)
1. Swift, Jonathan
I. Title II. McMinn, Joseph III. Series
828.509

ISBN 0–86140–297–9
ISBN 0–86140–328–2 pbk ✓

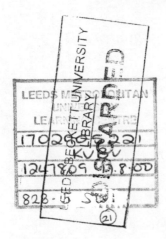
Produced in Great Britain
Printed and bound by Billing & Sons Ltd., Worcester

For Andrew Carpenter

CONTENTS

A NOTE ON THE SELECTION
AND ANNOTATION

The following selection tries to illustrate the range of Swift's views on Ireland through texts which span his entire writing-career. I have naturally included a sample of those classic pamphlets, *The Drapier's Letters* and *A Modest Proposal*, which helped immortalise him as 'Hibernian Patriot' and savage ironist. But the other texts in the selection, less well-known ones, should be considered just as typical of his reflections on Ireland. Taken together, they try to show the practical and materialistic character of Swift's pamphleteering spirit. The pamphlet is essentially a form of appeal, and Swift was permanently concerned to publicise Ireland's chronic condition. But that appeal, as the selection shows, was nearly always made anonymously or pseudonymously. Only when speaking from the pulpit in St. Patrick's was such disguise irrelevant. It is extremely rare to hear Swift speaking in his own voice, which is why I have included the text of one of his polemical sermons on Irish affairs. This selection, I hope, will remind us that Swift's fundamental loyalty was to his Church and birthplace, and that their survival was the real business of most of his literary enterprise.

A most striking aspect of Swift's pamphlets is the problematic nature of the form itself. There is an extraordinary variety to the shape and purpose of this medium, as practised by Swift. What is usually regarded as the dominant characteristic of the pamphlet, a short polemic of a public nature, is only part of the story in this case. Swift's pamphlets function as propaganda, epistle, tract, broadside, advertisement, allegory, manifesto, petition, essay, memorandum and manual. The outstanding and deserved reputation of *The Drapier's Letters* should not encourage us to take their form as the definitive mode of the Swiftian pamphlet. The evidence is testimony to great variety and adaptability of skills.

Many of Swift's pamphlets were composed without regard to immediate publication. Nearly a third of them were unpublished in his lifetime, nearly always because he did not consider them of adequate literary importance, or because the occasion was politically inappropriate. Often, they were finally published because a printer,

9

like Faulkner, wanted to make money out of the name of the Drapier. Almost half the contemporary or final publication of the Irish writings were the work of two Dublin printers, John Harding and George Faulkner. John and Sarah Harding published thirteen pieces, including some of the most renowned, such as *A Modest Proposal*. Faulkner printed twenty-seven, making him indeed the 'Prince of Dublin Printers', as Swift called him. More significantly, Faulkner's name was to be forever associated with the first Dublin edition of Swift's *Works*, in four volumes, which he printed in 1735, while the ageing Dean was well enough and willing to assist.

The texts in this selection are based on Faulkner and subsequent editions of Swift's writings. Because of Swift's personal interest in Faulkner's first edition, these originals retain considerable authority. There were occasional omissions and errors, however, which have been restored and amended in the present selection. Swift's original typography, especially his aggressive and rhythmical use of italics and full capitals for key-words and names, has been retained. Without it, the distinctive visual dimension to his literary rhetoric would be lost.

Facing the opening page of each pamphlet, I have supplied a short paragraph which gives details of original composition and publication, when known, and a few comments on essential context. Working alongside Faulkner, Swift himself provided some annotation and introductory commentary: these have been retained, and are easily distinguishable by their use of asterisks in the place of numbers. My own annotation is limited to those allusions and remarks by Swift which the modern reader may need to understand to appreciate more fully the historical context of the writing. It is always tempting to say too much, but that would be a distraction from, and not an invitation to, the narrative rhythm of the texts.

The standard edition of Swift's prose writings is *The Prose Works of Jonathan Swift*, edited by Herbert Davis, 14 Vols., Oxford, Blackwell, 1939–68. Two additional volumes, XV and XVI, which contain *The Journal to Stella*, have since been added and complete the set. For those with a special interest in the Irish pamphlets, the relevant volumes in this edition provide valuable historical and bibliographical commentary. No editor of Swift could work without the meticulous assistance of Davis.

I would like to thank Robert Welch and John McVeagh, my editors, for patient and instructive help. For some points of literary detective-work, my thanks to Ronnie Bailie, Dave Archard, Alan Peacock, and especially to Michael McGann, Estelle Haan and Frederick Williams of Queen's University Belfast. David Woolley, gentleman and scholar, gave me the practical benefit of his worthy experience of editing Swift. I would also like to record my thanks to Eric Saunders, Chairman of the University of Ulster Academic Publications Committee, the staff of Marsh's Library, the National Library of Ireland, the British Library, the Linenhall Library, and the University of Ulster Library. Finally, this work was given generous financial assistance from the British Academy and the Research Sub-Committee of the Faculty of Humanities in the University of Ulster.

INTRODUCTION

Swift's direct involvement with Ireland, as writer and clergyman, is dramatically illustrated through the many pamphlets he wrote on public and national affairs. From his instalment as Dean of St. Patrick's Cathedral in 1713, until his death in 1745, he wrote over sixty pamphlets on a range of issues, including major questions of Church and State, economic reform, famine and poverty, and the continual problem of Ireland's constitutional relation to England. This substantial and eloquent career has been overshadowed by critical preference for Swift's major satires, *A Tale of a Tub* (1704), and *Gulliver's Travels* (1726), both of which were written for a specific London audience. This reputation as a satirist of an essential and universal human nature is based on a view of Swift as a writer whose vision transcends parochial and contemporary pressures of his day. Such a selection often yields quite an abstract image of Swift, and neglects his life-long commentary on Irish realities. The present selection of Swift's pamphlets reveals a writer intensely concerned with material, everyday issues in eighteenth century Ireland. There may well have been a concept of universal Man and an essential human nature which made all local variations of negligible interest, but the pamphlets tell a complementary story. They testify to Swift's lasting concern with the immediate, concrete and tangible affairs of a country in continual crisis.

Swift's writings on Ireland are based on the belief that literature of this kind was a public service, vital to the civil and social improvement of the State. They are, like most pamphlets, rhetorical exercises in the art of persuasion. Polemical and functional, their purpose is to change influential attitudes on issues of national importance, so that Ireland will be a saner and more civilised place for its people. Despite their eloquence, they show no interest in literary immortality: yet, because of their artful design and dramatic character, they tell us a great deal about Swift's Ireland and its early colonial literature. An appreciation of the pamphlets' role and intention also gives us a clearer picture of Swift as a "committed" writer, broadens our understanding of the social dimension of such literature, and illustrates the political origins of the Anglo-Irish tradition.

Pamphlets were central to open political debate in both England and Ireland during the eighteenth century. Immediately before taking up the Deanery of St. Patrick's, Swift had reached the heights of political power in England through his services as pamphleteer and propagandist for the Tory ministry, using his polemical powers to justify government policies on the constitution and foreign affairs. By this time, he had written little about Ireland, since he never intended or wished to return there. Once the Whigs came to power in 1714, and Swift reluctantly accepted the Dublin post, his Irish career comes into proper perspective. In a sense, Ireland forced Swift into her cause. After an initial indifference and silence, he took up his pen on behalf of Ireland and was soon to become, through his outspoken pamphlets, a popular national figure.

Above all else, Swift's pamphlets represent a defence of "the Protestant interest" in Ireland. They consistently, though regretfully, raise the legal and constitutional rights of what Swift saw as a supremely loyal but unjustly treated part of his Majesty's Kingdom. Swift resented and rejected any suggestion that Ireland was a colony. This protest was begun years beforehand, in 1698, by William Molyneux, a Dublin M.P. and founder of the Dublin Philosophical Society. Molyneux had written a controversial pamphlet, *The Case of Ireland being bound by Acts of Parliament in England, Stated*, in which he insisted on the legal autonomy of the Irish parliament under the Crown. The *Case*, immediately charged with sedition, became the guiding principle of Swift's pamphlets on this crucial issue. In 1724, at the height of the Wood's half-pence controversy when Swift assumed the disguise of a Dublin Drapier to argue against the introduction of debased and unwanted coinage into the Irish economy, he declared:

It is true, indeed, that within the Memory of Man, the Parliaments of England have sometimes assumed the Power of binding this Kingdom, by Laws enacted there: wherein they were, at first, openly opposed (as far as Truth, Reason, and Justice are capable of opposing) by the famous Mr. Molineaux, an English Gentleman born here; as well as by several of the greatest Patriots, and best Whigs in England; but the Love and Torrent of Power prevailed. Indeed, the Arguments on both Sides were invincible. For in Reason, all Government without the Consent of the Governed, is the very Definition of Slavery.   (*To the Whole People of Ireland*, 1724)

Despite such indignant and righteous protest, the Declaratory Act of 1720 had already re-enforced London's claim to executive and legal control over Ireland.

In the same year as the Declaratory Act, Swift had produced his first pamphlet on Irish affairs since becoming Dean, *A Proposal for*

the Universal Use of Irish Manufacture, arguing for a boycott of
English goods as a way of encouraging a more self-reliant Irish
economy. It was promptly charged as seditious, although the case
was finally dropped.

When such practical proposals were charged as criminal, it only
served to strengthen Swift's insistence on Ireland's constitutional
integrity, and to refine his distinction between loyalty to the Crown
and submission to the parliament and politicians of the day. Four
years later, *To the Whole People of Ireland* was also charged as
treasonable and seditious. The government's determination to cen-
sor Irish pamphlets on the constitutional question was met with scorn
and anger by Swift, who felt increasingly alienated from English
politics. No matter how he idealised the Crown and Constitution,
he could not promise unconditional loyalty so long as Protestants
were treated with such disregard. The difficult, because ambiguous,
situation of Protestant Ireland forced Swift to criticise those very
institutions he most admired.

Swift's experience in England, where the ideal and the practice of
a public literature seemed to harmonize, fuelled his outrage at the
treatment of public opinion in Ireland. He asserted, not very con-
vincingly, that whereas London welcomed pamphleteers, Dublin
viewed them as subversive. Writing as the Drapier to Viscount
Molesworth, Swift remarks on the shock of experiencing such
double-standards:

. . . this Habit of Writing and Discoursing, wherein I unfortunately differ
from almost the whole Kingdom, and am apt to grate the Ears of more than
I could wish; was acquired during my Apprenticeship in London, and a long
Residence there after I had set up for my self. Upon my Return and Settlement here, I thought I had only changed one Country of Freedom for
another.   (*To Viscount Molesworth,* 1724)

This is a favourite note of the pamphlets — a mock-innocent dis-
appointment and surprise. Swift knew well that Ireland was a
dangerous place for the public-spirited writer. That is why so many
pamphlets were produced anonymously or expressed the views of
a fictional persona. Whatever the threat, Swift refused to be silent,
seeing his role as a writer in terms of public duty and Christian
conscience.

There is an evangelical quality to Swift's pamphlets which reminds
us that this writer is also a clergyman in the Church of Ireland, and
a figure of authority in its hierarchy. This is the Church established
by the law, the State Church, as Swift repeatedly points out to its
critics and dissenters. Respect for ecclesiastical authority is also a

public duty and responsibility, and this often conditions the rhetoric of the pamphlets. To speak for the State Church meant that politics, law and theology were inseparable. Just as Swift defends the colonial Protestant interest in Ireland against such political misrule, so he defends the Church against all attempts to question or dilute its authority as the voice of God. Moves by the Whig government to encourage legal toleration for Protestant dissenters, especially Presbyterians, were stoutly and stubbornly resisted by Swift. The loyal Protestants of the Church of Ireland had enough political problems without encouraging those bent on further damage to the unity of Church and State. Penal laws, he felt, were the just deserts of those who threatened such uniformity. At the same time, Swift was equally fierce in his criticism of English place-men in the Irish hierarchy, men who merely echoed government policy in the hope of promotion and refused to acknowledge Ireland's chronic situation for fear of disfavour. In religion as in politics, Swift opposed any kind of arbitrary rule which was not based on the consent of those loyal to the unity of Church and State. This, of course, was the guiding principle of the English constitution after the defeat of King James. But Swift saw no evidence that it was being enforced in Ireland. Irish Protestants felt they represented the conscience of that constitutional pact. After all, Swift argued, Ireland was where the original tyranny was defeated, and where freedom by consent was achieved. Just as the clergyman had to steer his flock along the narrow path of conservative authority, so had the pamphleteer to speak out in the name of conscience to protect his people from injustice and betrayal. Priest and writer shared the same vocation.

Proof of Swift's recognition of the primacy of material issues in Ireland is seen in the number of pamphlets dominated by the economy. Like many others, Swift viewed Ireland's critical economic plight as unnecessary and unnatural, and proposed many practical reforms. Much of Ireland's problem he attributed directly to unfair, protective legislation by England which prevented competition from Ireland. As a partial but effective means of escape from that control and dependency, Swift urged the boycott of English goods and a greater consumption of home-made manufactures. This was an early version of a "Buy-Irish" campaign in the name of self-reliance. Such a campaign, argued Swift, would also challenge the slavish assumption that everything Irish was naturally inferior. The normal rules of a healthy economy — a large and growing population, unique natural resources, freedom of economic traffic — never seemed to apply to Ireland in practice. Famine was common, tillage was neglected in favour of pasture, beggary was universal. These appeals for reform went largely unheeded.

Swift despaired of progress and summarised Ireland's absurd economic condition — "There is not one Argument used to prove the Riches of Ireland, which is not a logical Demonstration of its Poverty." His most famous pamphlet on the human economy, *A Modest Proposal* (1729), represents the climax of accumulated rage and frustration. Seen in the overall context of Swift's many pamphlets on the economy, it is also an extraordinary piece of self-parody. Faced with a national crisis, well-intentioned reforms begin to sound increasingly ludicrous. Polite philanthropy is now a conventional form of national madness. The pamphlet's ironic distortions of earlier proposals by Swift mark a pessimism from which Swift never fully recovered. Such scorn is fatal to a form of writing which assumes the possibility of change and improvement. The pamphlets on the Irish economy expose a humiliating dilemma — Ireland can only prosper if she has political control over her own affairs: since Ireland cannot secure that control, reform is a waste of time.

In 1724, masked as the Drapier, Swift was a popular writer, widely-read throughout the country. By the end of that decade he felt little enthusiasm for pamphleteering:

> I am tired with Letters from many unreasonable well-meaning People, who are daily pressing me to deliver my Thoughts in this deplorable Juncture, which upon many others I have so often done in vain. What will it import that half a score of people in a Coffee-house may happen to read this paper, and even the Majority of those few differ in every sentiment from me.
>
> (*Answer to Several Letters from Unknown Persons*, 1729)

No great public or national issue comparable to that of Wood's half-pence presented itself to Swift after 1724, although he continued to campaign on public affairs until his last years. Instead, Swift turned wearily away from constitutional and economic reforms to more personal and ecclesiastical topics. A public literature like pamphleteering is often at the mercy of changing times and moods.

Who read these pamphlets? One way of answering this question about Swift's society is to note the varied and clearly-defined audiences he addressed. The pamphlets are supremely conscious of class in society — the Catholic peasantry, representatives of the Crown, artisans, farmers, landlords, various levels of the Church hierarchy, women of fashion, servants, politicians and businessmen. Swift has little tolerance for the extremes of poverty and wealth, regarding both as equally ignorant and hopeless. His political sympathies lie with the Church of Ireland "middle Rank", those with enough property to come within his stern definition of responsible citizenship. The pamphlets, especially *The Drapier's Letters*, aspire to a "national" audience. This aspiration is largely rhetorical, a tactic designed to lend authority to the writer's arguments by identifying a part of the nation as the authentic voice of the whole people. In reality, the pamphlets were distributed to a small section of the Anglican community in Dublin, and to sympathetic friends in the country, often clergymen and teachers. Swift was not in a position to write for "The Whole People of Ireland". In such a fractured society, still recovering from the changes of 1690, spokesmen like Swift were inevitably the voice of a sectional interest. His is a colonial voice which aspires, in a paternalistic way, towards a broader and simpler sense of nationhood which would unite the interests of all classes under the authority of a single Church and State. It is, evidently, a feudal outlook.

Swift's care with audience and style shows what an able rhetorician lies behind the pamphlets. Their characteristic style, no matter what audience is addressed, is magisterial but direct, formal yet energetic. Formality of this kind has a political source which finds an appropriate literary tone. It derives from Swift's sense of the dignity of his cause, no matter how his ideals of government and society are negated by contemporary practice. On the other hand, the pamphlets have a job to do. They never forget to focus clearly on the chosen target, and are exemplary exercises in direct appeal. They show a restless and observant view of contemporary Ireland, and an impatient need to bring people to their senses. For Swift, a pamphlet reveals the obvious. As the Drapier puts it:

> . . . the boldest and most obnoxious Words I ever delivered, would in England have only exposed me as a stupid Fool, who went to prove that the Sun shone in a clear Summer's Day.   (*To Viscount Molesworth, 1724*)

Unquestioning loyalty by Irish Protestants was a form of blindness and dishonesty which Swift would not tolerate, even at the risk of being charged with disloyalty. As writer and clergyman he plays the role of a people's moral custodian. He must, therefore, find a common style without compromising an authoritative one. That is why the judicial, at times surgical, manner of the pamphlets is leavened by repeated use of anecdote and dramatic visual imagery. The crisis of inflation is dramatised in imaginary scenes of ludicrous personal effort to pay for a pint of beer with a cartload of debased coins. The systematic rhetorical order of *A Modest Proposal* finds a simil ~ stylistic concreteness in its imagery of children prepared "hot from the Knife". No pamphlet succeeds just because of its argument: it must also appeal to the imagination.

Swift's pamphlets ensured his contemporary reputation as the

"Hibernian Patriot". The Dean's birthday was celebrated publicly every November, the weavers and drapiers of his parish in the "Liberties" of Dublin made him a popular hero for his efforts on behalf of their trade, and he was granted the freedom of the City in Dublin and Cork. Even today, Swift as pamphleteer is the literary basis of the political legend which views Swift as modern Ireland's first patriotic writer. Some of this is the result of an imaginative need on the part of later generations to see Swift as the father of Irish nationalism and his crusading pamphlets as the early critical weapons in the struggle for nationhood. In 1782, Henry Grattan addressed an Irish parliament which had finally repealed the Declaratory Act, and saluted the Dean as the imaginative architect of Irish legislative independence:

I found Ireland on her knees, I watched over her with a paternal solicitude: I have traced her progress from injuries to arms, and from arms to liberty. Spirit of Swift! Spirit of Molyneux! Your genius has prevailed. Ireland is now a nation.

Retrospectively, Grattan was paying tribute to the creators of the Anglo-Irish identity, a special form of constitutional patriotism. Swift provided a symbol of heroic, eloquent and dignified resistance to injustice. In his "Introduction" to *The Words upon the Window Pane* (1934), a play about that same spirit of Swift, W. B. Yeats defines a similarly heroic image of the Dean:

It was this doctrine that Swift uttered in the *Fourth Drapier's Letter* with such astringent eloquence that it passed from the talk of study and parlour to that of road and market, and created the political nationality of Ireland.

Swift's pamphlets are fundamental to the rhetoric of the Anglo-Irish literary and political tradition. The rhetoric of liberty, largely derived from the writings of John Locke, always sounds expansive and absolute even if the application is selective and conditional. Swift's patriotism is real, but it belongs to eighteenth-century Ireland not to modern romantic nationalism. It is based solidly on the idea of public service. It is conservative but critical, against useless change but forever demanding improvement. The pamphlets expose many contradictions of the colonial relation with England, but they can never envisage a resolution of those contradictions.

To a great extent the frustration which motivates the pamphlets reflects the tensions within Ireland at the time. Swift's writings implied the need for radical change, but dreaded the prospect. His Protestantism held itself up as the supreme example of stoic loyalty, but was forever dissatisfied. Caught between roles of mastery and servitude, loyalty and betrayal, it struggled for some liberating sense of identity based on consensus and freedom. The rhetoric was usually heroic, but the reality was often farcical. The importance of Swift's Irish pamphlets lies in their original expression of these contradictions and aspirations — forces born out of unease and confusion.

THE
STORY
OF THE
INJURED LADY.

WRITTEN by HERSELF.

In a LETTER to her FRIEND, with
his ANSWER.

This political allegory was Swift's first pamphlet on Irish affairs. Written in 1707, (but not published until 1746), it was provoked by the constitutional union between England and Scotland. Swift felt that loyal, Protestant Ireland had been betrayed in favour of dissenting, Presbyterian Scotland. His bitter rejection of Ireland's 'dependent' or colonial status, first stated here, remained central to his understanding of Anglo-Irish relations.

THE
STORY
OF THE
INJURED LADY.

WRITTEN by HERSELF.

In a LETTER to her FRIEND, with
his ANSWER.

SIR,

BEING ruined by the Inconstancy and Unkindness of a Lover, I
hope, a true and plain Relation of my Misfortunes may be of Use
and Warning to credulous Maids, never to put too much Trust in
deceitful Men.

A Gentleman in the Neighbourhood had two Mistresses, another
and myself; and he pretended honourable Love to us both. Our three
Houses stood pretty near one another; his was parted from mine
by a River, and from my Rival's by an old broken Wall. But before
I enter into the Particulars of this Gentleman's hard Usage of me,
I will give a very just and impartial Character of my Rival and
myself.

As to her Person, she is tall and lean, and very ill-shaped; she
hath bad Features, and a worse Complexion; she hath a stinking
Breath, and twenty ill Smells about her besides, which are yet more
unsufferable by her natural Sluttishness; for she is always lousy, and
never without the Itch. As to her other Qualities, she hath no Reputation either for Virtue, Honesty, Truth, or Manners; and it is no
Wonder, considering what her Education hath been. Scolding and
Cursing are her common Conversation. To sum up all, she is poor
and beggarly, and getteth a sorry Maintenance by pilfering where
ever she cometh. As for this Gentleman who is now so fond of her,
she still beareth him an invincible Hatred; revileth him to his Face,
and raileth at him in all Companies. Her House is frequented by a
Company of Rogues and Thieves, and Pickpockets, whom she
encourageth to rob his Hen-roosts, steal his Corn and Cattle, and

do him all manner of Mischief. She hath been known to come at the Head of these Rascals, and beat her Lover until he was sore from Head to Foot, and then force him to pay for the Trouble she was at. Once, attended with a Crew of Raggamuffins, she broke into his House, turned all Things topsy-turvy, and then set it on Fire. At the same Time she told so many Lies among his Servants, that it set them all by the Ears, and his poor Steward was knocked on the Head; for which, I think, and so doth all the Country, that she ought to be answerable. To conclude her Character; she is of a different Religion, being a Presbyterian of the most rank and virulent Kind, and consequently having an inveterate Hatred to the Church; yet, I am sure, I have been always told, that in Marriage there ought to be an Union of Minds as well as of Persons.

I will now give my own Character; and shall do it in few Words, and with Modesty and Truth.

I was reckoned to be as handsome as any in our Neighbourhood, until I became pale and thin with Grief and ill Usage. I am still fair enough, and have, I think, no very ill Feature about me. They that see me now, will hardly allow me ever to have had any great Share of Beauty; for, besides being so much altered, I go always mobbed, and in an Undress, as well out of Neglect, as indeed for want of Cloaths to appear in. I might add to all this, that I was born to a good Estate, although it now turneth to little Account, under the Oppressions I endure; and hath been the true Cause of all my Misfortunes.

Some Years ago, this Gentleman, taking a Fancy either to my Person or Fortune, made his Addresses to me; which, being then young and foolish, I too readily admitted; he seemed to use me with so much Tenderness, and his Conversation was so very engaging, that all my Constancy and Virtue were too soon overcome; and, to dwell no longer upon a Theme that causeth such bitter Reflections, I must confess, with Shame, that I was undone by the common Arts practised upon all easy credulous Virgins, half by Force, and half by Consent, after solemn Vows and Protestations of Marriage. When he had once got Possession, he soon began to play the usual Part of a too fortunate Lover, affecting, on all Occasions, to shew his Authority, and to act like a Conqueror. First, he found Fault with the Government of my Family, which, to grant, was none of the best, consisting of ignorant, illiterate Creatures; for, at that Time, I knew but little of the World. In Compliance to him, therefore, I agreed to fall into his Ways and Methods of Living,[1] I consented that his Steward should govern my House,

---

1 In the following lines, Swift sets out the system of rule whereby the 'Steward', the English Monarch, governs Ireland through an 'Under-Steward', the Lord Lieutenant, who often appointed pro-English placemen to all positions of influence and power. The Lady acknowledges, however, that this was originally done with her consent: it is the abuse of the arrangement, and not the arrangement itself, which outrages her.

and have Liberty to employ an Under-Steward, who should receive his Directions. My Lover proceeded further, turning away several old Servants and Tenants, and supplying me with others from his own House. These grew so domineering and unreasonable, that there was no Quiet; and I heard of nothing but perpetual Quarrels, which, although I could not possibly help, yet my Lover laid all the Blame and Punishment upon me; and, upon every Falling-out, still turned away more of my People, and supplied me in their Stead with a Number of Fellows and Dependents of his own, whom he had no other Way to provide for. Overcome by Love, and to avoid Noise and Contention, I yielded to all his Usurpations; and finding it in vain to resist, I thought it my best Policy to make my Court to my new Servants, and draw them to my Interests; I fed them from my own Table with the best I had; put my new Tenants on the choice Parts of my Land, and treated them all so kindly, that they began to love me as well as their Master. In Process of Time, all my old Servants were gone, and I had not a Creature about me, nor above one or two Tenants, but what were of his chusing; yet I had the good Luck, by gentle Usage, to bring over the greatest Part of them to my Side. When my Lover observed this, he began to alter his Language; and, to those who enquired about me, he would answer, that I was an old Dependent upon his Family, whom he had placed on some Concerns of his own; and he began to use me accordingly, neglecting, by Degrees, all common civility in his Behaviour. I shall never forget the Speech he made me one Morning, which he delivered with all the Gravity in the World. He put me in Mind of the vast Obligations I lay under to him, in sending me so many of his People for my own Good, and to teach me Manners; that, it had cost him ten Times more than I was worth, to maintain me; that, it had been much better for him, if I had been damned, or burnt, or sunk to the Bottom of the Sea; that, it was but reasonable I should strain myself, as far as I was able, to reimburse him some of his Charges; that, from henceforward, he expected his Word should be a Law to me in all Things; that, I must maintain a Parish-watch against Thieves and Robbers, and give Salaries to an Overseer, a Constable, and others, all of his own chusing, whom he would send, from Time to Time, to be Spies upon me; that, to enable me the better in supporting these Expences, my Tenants should be obliged to carry all their Goods cross the River to his Town-market, and pay Toll on both Sides, and then sell them at half Value: But, because we were a nasty Sort of People, and that he could not endure to touch any Thing we had a Hand in, and likewise, because he wanted Work to employ his own Folks, therefore, we must send all our Goods to his Market, just in their Naturals;[2] the Milk immediately from the Cow, without making it into Cheese or Butter; the Corn in the Ear; the Grass as it is mowed; the Wool as it cometh from the Sheep's Back; and bring the Fruit upon the Branch, that he might not be obliged to eat it after our filthy Hands; that, if a Tenant carried but a Piece of Bread and Cheese to eat by the Way, or an Inch of Worsted to mend his Stockings, he should forfeit his whole Parcel; and, because a Company of Rogues usually plied on the River between us, who often robbed my Tenants of their Goods and Boats, he ordered a Waterman of his to guard them, whose Manner was to be out of the Way until the poor Wretches were plundered; then to overtake the Thieves, and seize all as lawful Prize to his Master and himself. It would be endless to repeat an hundred other Hardships he put upon me; but it is a general Rule, that whenever he imagines the smallest Advantage will redound to one of his Footboys, by any new Oppression of me and my whole Family and Estate, he never disputeth it a Moment. All this hath rendered me so very insignificant and contemptible at Home, that some Servants to whom I pay the greatest Wages, and many Tenants who have the most beneficial Leases, are gone over to live with him; yet I am bound to continue their Wages, and pay their Rents; by which Means one Third Part of my whole Income is spent on his Estate, and above another Third by his Tolls and Markets; and my poor Tenants are so sunk and impoverished, that, instead of maintaining me suitable to my Quality, they can hardly find me Cloaths to keep me warm, or provide the common Necessaries of Life for themselves.

Matters being in this Posture between me and my Lover, I received Intelligence, that he had been for some Time making very pressing Overtures of Marriage to my Rival, until there happened some Misunderstandings between them; she gave him ill Words, and threatened to break off all Commerce with him. He, on the other Side, having either acquired Courage by his Triumphs over me, or supposing her as tame a Fool as I, thought at first to carry it with an high Hand; but hearing, at the same Time, that she had Thoughts of making some private Proposals to join with me against him, and doubting, with very good Reason, that I would readily accept them, he seemed very much disconcerted. This, I thought, was a proper Occasion to shew some great Example of Generosity and Love; and so, without further Consideration, I sent him Word, that hearing

2 An allusion to economic legislation, especially the Woollen Act of 1699, whereby England prohibited Ireland from exporting manufactured goods in competition with English trading interests.

there was like to be a Quarrel between him and my Rival, notwithstanding all that had passed, and without binding him to any Conditions in my own Favour, I would stand by him against her and all the World, while I had a Penny in my Purse, or a Petticoat to pawn. This Message was subscribed by all my chief Tenants; and proved so powerful, that my Rival immediately grew more tractable upon it. The Result of which was, that there is now a Treaty of Marriage concluded between them, the Wedding Cloaths are bought, and nothing remaineth but to perform the Ceremony, which is put off for some Days, because they design it to be a publick Wedding. And, to reward my Love, Constancy, and Generosity, he hath bestowed on me the Office of being Sempstress to his Grooms and Footmen, which I am forced to accept, or starve; yet, in the Midst of this my Situation, I cannot but have some Pity for this deluded Man, to cast himself away on an infamous Creature, who, whatever she pretendeth, I can prove, would, at this very Minute, rather be a Whore to a certain great Man,[3] that shall be nameless, if she might have her Will. For my Part, I think, and so doth all the Country too, that the Man is possessed; at least none of us are able to imagine what he can possibly see in her, unless she hath bewitched him, or given him some Powder.

I am sure, I never sought his Alliance; and you can bear me Witness, that I might have had other Matches; nay, if I were lightly disposed, I could still, perhaps, have Offers, that some, who hold their Heads higher, would be glad to accept. But, alas! I never had any such wicked Thought; all I now desire is, only to enjoy a little Quiet, to be free from the Persecutions of this unreasonable Man, and that he will let me manage my own little Fortune to the best Advantage; for which I will undertake to pay him a considerable Pension every Year, much more considerable than what he now getteth by his Oppressions; for he must needs find himself a Loser at last, when he hath drained me and my Tenants so dry, that we shall not have a Penny for him, or ourselves. There is one Imposition of his, I had almost forgot, which I think unsufferable, and will appeal to you, or any reasonable Person, whether it be so or not. I told you before, that by an old Compact, we agreed to have the same Steward, at which Time I consented likewise to regulate my Family and Estate by the same Method with him, which he then shewed me, writ down in Form, and I approved of it. Now, the Turn he thinketh fit to give this Compact of ours is very extraordinary; for he pretendeth, that whatever Orders he shall think fit to prescribe for the future in his Family, he may, if he will, compel mine to

3 The Stuart Pretender.

observe them, without asking my Advice, or hearing my Reasons; so that I must not make a Lease without his Consent, or give any Direction for the well-governing of my Family, but what he countermandeth whenever he pleaseth. This leaveth me at such Confusion and Uncertainty, that my Servants know not when to obey me, and my Tenants, although many of them be very well inclined, seem quite at a Loss.

But, I am too tedious upon this melancholy Subject, which, however, I hope, you will forgive, since the Happiness of my whole Life dependeth upon it. I desire you will think a while, and give me your best Advice what Measures I shall take with Prudence, Justice, Courage, and Honour, to protect my Liberty and Fortune against the Hardships and Severities I lie under from that unkind, inconstant Man.

A
LETTER

FROM A

MEMBER

OF THE

House of Commons

IN

IRELAND

TO A

MEMBER

OF THE

House of Commons

IN

ENGLAND,

Concerning the *Sacramental TEST.*

Written in the YEAR *1708*

This *Letter*, in which Swift adopts the character of an Irish M.P., was written in 1708, and first published in the following year. As a Church of Ireland priest, he consistently opposed legal toleration of Dissent, but especially of Ulster Presbyterians. The 'Test' legally required all those not of the Established Church to formally recognise its absolute authority. The religious and political threat posed by Dissent was a life-long obsession of Swift, and this pamphlet was reprinted several times during his career. However self-contradictory from a modern, liberal viewpoint, his conservative resistance to toleration was a cardinal and consistent principle.

THE
Publisher's Advertisement
TO THE
READER

IN the second Volume of Doctor *Swift's* and Mr. *Pope's* Miscellanies, I found the following Treatise, which had been printed in *London*, with some other of the *Dean's* Works many Years before, but at first came out by it self in the Year 1708, as the Date shews: And it was at a Juncture, when the *Dissenters* were endeavouring to repeal the *Sacramental Test*, as by common Fame, and some Pamphlets published to the same Purpose, they seem to be now again attempting, with great Hope of Success. I have, therefore, taken the Liberty to make an Extract out of that Discourse, omitting only some Passages, which relate to certain Persons, and are of no Consequence to the Argument. But the Author's Way of Reasoning seems at present to have more Weight, than it had in those Times, when the Discourse first appeared.

The Author, in this Letter, personates a Member of Parliament here, to a Member of Parliament in *England*.

The Speaker mentioned in this Letter was *Allen Broderick*, afterwards Chancellor and Lord *Middleton*; and the Prelate was Dr. *Lindsay*, afterwards Lord Primate.

A
LETTER

FROM A

MEMBER

OF THE

House of Commons

OF

IRELAND, &c.

SIR,

I RECEIVED your Letter, wherein you tell me of the strange Representations made of us on your Side of the Water. The Instance you are
pleased to mention, is that of the Presbyterian *Missionary*, who,
according to your Phrase, hath been lately *persecuted* in *Drogheda*
for his Religion; but it is easy to observe, how mighty industrious
some People have been for three or four Years past, to hand about
Stories of the Hardships, the Merits, the Number, and the Power
of the *Presbyterians* in *Ireland*, to raise formidable Ideas of the
Dangers of *Popery* there, and to transmit all for *England*, improved
by great Additions, and with special Care to have them inserted,
with Comments, in those infamous weekly Papers that infest your
Coffee Houses. So, when the Clause enacting a *Sacramental Test*
was put in Execution, it was given out in *England*, that half the
Justices of Peace through this Kingdom had laid down their Commissions; whereas, upon Examination, the whole Number was found
to amount only to a Dozen or Thirteen, and those generally of the
lowest Rate in Fortune and Understanding, and some of them
superannuated. So, when the Earl of *Pembroke* was in *Ireland*, and
the Parliament sitting, a formal Story was very gravely carried to
his Excellency by some zealous Members, of a Priest newly arrived,

from Abroad, to the *North-West* Parts of *Ireland*, who had publickly preached to his People, to fall a murthering the Protestants; which Abuse, although invented to serve an End they were then upon, and are still driving at, was presently handed over, and printed with shrewd Remarks by your worthy Scriblers. In like Manner, the Account of that Person, who was lately expelled our University for reflecting on the Memory of King *William*, what a Dust it raised, and how foully it was related, is fresh enough in Memory. Neither would People be convinced till the University was at the Pains of publishing a *Latin* Paper to justify themselves. And, to mention no more, this Story of the *Persecution* at *Drogheda*, how it hath been spread and aggravated, what Consequences drawn from it, and what Reproaches fixed on those who have least deserved them, we are already informed. Now, if the End of all this Proceeding were a Secret and Mystery, I should not pretend to give it an Interpretation. But sufficient Care hath been taken to explain it. First, by Addresses artificially (if not illegally) procured, to shew the miserable State of the Dissenters in *Ireland*, by reason of the *Sacramental Test*, and to desire the Queen's Intercession that it might be repealed. Then it is manifest, that our * Speaker, when he was last Year in *England*, sollicited, in Person, several Members of both Houses, to have it repealed by an Act there, although it be a Matter purely national, that cannot possibly interfere with the Trade and Interest of *England*, and although he himself appeared formerly the most zealous of all Men against the Injustice of binding a Nation by Laws, to which they do not consent.[1] And lastly, those weekly Libellers, whenever they get a Tale by the End relating to *Ireland*, without once troubling their Thoughts about the Truth, always end it with an Application against the *Sacramental Test*, and the absolute Necessity there is of repealing it in both Kingdoms. I know it may be reckoned a Weakness to say any thing of such Trifles as are below a serious Man's Notice: Much less would I disparage the Understanding of any Party, to think they would choose the Vilest and most Ignorant among mankind, to employ them for Asserters of a Cause. I shall only say, that the scandalous Liberty those Wretches take, would hardly be allowed, if it were not mingled with Opinions that *some Men* would be glad to advance. Besides, how insipid so ever those Papers are, they seem to be levelled to the Understandings of a

---

* *Mr. Broderick*, afterwards Chancellor.

1 Allan Broderick (1660–1728), here castigated for his liberal views on toleration, became Lord Chancellor Middleton. In 1724, during the campaign against Wood's half-pence, Swift addressed one of the *Drapier's Letters* to him, praising his resistance to government without consent. See *Prose Works*, X, pp. 99–115.

great Number. They are grown a necessary Part in Coffee-house Furniture, and some Time or other happen to be read by Customers of all Ranks, for Curiosity or Amusement; because they lie always in the Way. One of these Authors (the Fellow that was * *pilloryed*, I have forgot his Name) is indeed so grave, sententious, dogmatical a Rogue, that there is no enduring him; the *Observator*² is much the brisker of the two; and, I think, farther gone of late in Lies and Impudence than his *Presbyterian* Brother.

I now come to answer the other Part of your Letter, and shall give you my Opinion freely about repealing the *Sacramental Test*; only, whereas you desire my Thoughts as a Friend, and not as I am a Member of Parliament, I must assure you they are exactly the same in both Capacities.

I must begin by telling you, we are generally surprised at your wonderful Kindness to us on this Occasion, in being so very industrious to teach us to see our Interests, in a Point where we are so unable to see it our selves. This hath given us some Suspicion; and although, in my own Particular, I am hugely bent to believe, that whenever you concern your selves in our Affairs, it is certainly *for our Good*; yet I have the Misfortune to be something singular in this Belief, and therefore I never attempted to justify it, but content my self to possess my own Opinion in private, for fear of encountring Men of more Wit, or Words than I have to spare.

We at this Distance, who see nothing of the Spring of Actions, are forced, by mere Conjecture, to assign two Reasons for your desiring us to repeal the *Sacramental Test*. One is, because you are said to imagine it will be a Step towards the like *good Work* in *England*: The other more immediate, that it will open a Way for rewarding *several Persons*, who have well deserved upon a *great Occasion*, but who are now unqualified through that Impediment.

I do not frequently quote Poets, especially *English*, but I remember there is in some of Mr. *Cowley's* Love Verses,³ a Strain that I thought extraordinary at Fifteen, and have often since imagined it to be spoken by *Ireland*.

> *Forbid it Heaven my Life should be*
> *Weigh'd with her least Conveniency.*

In short, whatever Advantage you propose to your selves by

* *Daniel Defoe.*

2 *The Observator* was a contemporary Whig periodical, published in London by John Tutchin.

3 Abraham Cowley (1618–67), whose Pindaric Odes Swift imitated in his earliest verse.

repealing the *Sacramental Test*, speak it out plainly, it is the best Argument you can use, for we value your Interest much more than our own. If your little Finger be sore, and you think a Poultice made of our *Vitals* will give it any Ease, speak the Word, and it shall be done; the Interest of our whole Kingdom is, at any Time, ready to strike to that of your poorest *Fishing Towns*; it is hard you will not accept our Services, unless we believe, at the same Time, that you are only consulting our Profit, and giving us Marks of your Love. If there be a Fire at some Distance, and I immediately blow up my House before there be Occasion, because you are a Man of Quality, and apprehend some Danger to a *Corner of your Stable*; yet why should you require me to attend next Morning at your Levee, with my humble Thanks for the Favour you have done me?

If we might be allowed to judge for our selves, we had Abundance of Benefit by the *Sacramental Test*, and foresee a Number of Mischiefs would be the Consequence of repealing it; and we conceive the Objections made against it by the *Dissenters*, are of no Manner of Force: They tell us of their Merits in the late War in *Ireland*, and how chearfully they engaged for the Safety of the Nation; that if they had thought they were fighting only other Peoples Quarrels, perhaps it might have cooled their Zeal; and that, for the Future, they shall sit down quietly, and let us do our Work our selves; nay, that it is necessary they should do so, since they cannot take up Arms under the Penalty of High Treason.

Now, supposing them to have done their Duty, as I believe they did, and not to trouble them about the *Fly on the Wheel*; I thought *Liberty; Property*, and *Religion* had been the three Subjects of the Quarrel: And have not all those been amply secured to them? Had they, at that Time, a *mental Reservation* for *Power and Employments?* And must these two Articles be added henceforward in our National Quarrels? It is grown a mighty Conceit, among some Men, to melt down the Phrase of a *Church established by Law*, into that of *the Religion of the Magistrate*; of which Apellation it is easier to find the Reason than the Sense: If, by the *Magistrate*, they mean the *Prince*, the Expression includes a Falshood; for when King James was *Prince*, the Established Church was the same it is now: If, by the same Word they mean the Legislature, we desire no more. Be that as it will, we of this Kingdom believe the Church of *Ireland* to be the National Church, and the only one established by Law; and are willing, by the same Law, to give a *Toleration* to Dissenters. But if once we repeal our *Sacramental Test*, and grant a *Toleration*, or suspend the Execution of the Penal Laws, I do not see how we can be said to have any Established Church remaining; or rather why there will not be as many Established Churches as there are Sects of Dissenters. No, say they, yours will still be the National Church, because your Bishops and Clergy are maintained by the Publick; but, *That*, I suppose, will be of no long Duration, and it would be very unjust it should; because, to speak in *Tindal's* Phrase,[4] it is not reasonable that Revenues should be annexed to one Opinion more than another, when all are equally lawful; and it is the same Author's Maxim, That no free-born Subject ought to pay for maintaining Speculations he does not believe. *But why should any Man, upon Account of Opinions he cannot help, be deprived the Opportunity of serving his Queen and Country?* Their Zeal is commendable, and when Employments go a begging for want of Hands, they shall be sure to have the Refusal; only, upon Condition, that they will not pretend to them upon Maxims which equally include *Atheists, Turks, Jews, Infidels* and *Hereticks*; or which is still more dangerous, even *Papists* themselves; the former you allow, the other you deny, because these last own a foreign Power, and therefore must be shut out. But there is no great Weight in this; for their Religion can suit with free States, with limited or absolute Monarchies, as well as a better; and the *Pope's* Power in *France* is but a Shadow; so that, upon this Foot, there need be no great Danger to the Constitution, by admitting *Papists* to Employments. I will help you to enough of them, who shall be ready to allow the *Pope* as little Power here as you please; and the bare Opinion of his being Vicar of Christ, is but a *speculative Point*, for which no Man, it seems, ought to be deprived the Capacity of serving his Country.

But, if you please, I will tell you the great Objection we have against repealing this same *Sacramental Test*. It is, that we are verily perswaded the Consequence will be an entire Alteration of Religion among us, in a no great Compass of Years. And, pray observe, how we reason here in *Ireland* upon this Matter.

We observe the *Scots*, in our Northern Parts, to be an industrious People, extreamly devoted to their Religion, and full of an *undisturbed* Affection towards each other. Numbers of that *noble Nation*, invited by the Fertilities of the Soil, are glad to exchange their barren Hills of *Loughabar*, by a Voyage of three Hours, for our fruitful Vales of *Down* and *Antrim*, so productive of that *Grain*, which, at little Trouble and less Expence, finds Diet and Lodging for themselves and their Cattle. These People by their extream Parsimony, wonderful

---

4 Matthew Tindal (1657–1733), controversial deist and pamphleteer, author of *The Rights of the Christian Church Asserted* (1706). Swift saw him as the worst kind of anti-clerical freethinker, and attacked him in an unfinished, unpublished set of *Remarks*, written in 1707. See *Prose Works* II, pp. 68–80.

Dexterity in Dealing, and firm Adherence to one another, soon grow
into Wealth from the *smallest Beginnings*, never are rooted out where
they once fix, and increase daily by new Supplies. Besides, when
they are the superior Number in any Tract of Ground, they are not
over patient of Mixture; but such, whom they cannot *assimilate*, soon
find it their Interest to remove. I have done all in my Power, on
some Land of my own, to preserve two or three *English* Fellows in
their Neighbourhood, but found it impossible, although one of them
thought he had sufficiently made his Court by turning *Presbyterian*.
Add to all this, that they bring along with them from *Scotland*, a
most formidable Notion of our Church, which they look upon, at
least, three Degrees worse than *Popery*; and it is natural it should
be so, since they come over full fraught with that Spirit which taught
them to abolish Episcopacy at home.

Then we proceed farther, and observe, that the Gentlemen of
Employments here, make a very considerable Number in the House
of Commons, and have no *other Merit* but that of doing their Duty
in their several Stations; therefore, when the *Test* is repealed, it will
be highly reasonable they should give Place to those who have much
greater Services to plead. The Commissions of the Revenue are soon
disposed of, and the Collectors, and other Officers throughout the
Kingdom, are generally appointed by the Commissioners, which give
them a mighty Influence in every County. As much may be said of
the great Offices in the Law; and when this Door is open to let
Dissenters into the Commissions of the Peace, to make them High-
Sheriffs, Mayors of Corporations, and Officers of the Army and
Militia; I do not see how it can be otherwise, considering their
Industry and our Supineness, but that they may, in a very few Years,
grow to a Majority in the House of Commons, and consequently
make themselves the National Religion, and have a fair Pretence to
demand the Revenues of the Church for their Teachers. I know it
will be objected, that if all this should happen as I describe, yet the
Presbyterian Religion could never be made the National by Act of
Parliament, because our Bishops are so great a Number in the House
of Lords; and without a Majority there, the Church could not be
abolished. But I have *two very good Expedients* for that, which I
shall leave you to guess, and, I dare swear, our Speaker here has
often thought on, especially having endeavoured at *one of them* so
lately. That this Design is not so foreign from *some Peoples*
Thoughts, I must let you know what an honest* *Bell-weather* of our
House (you have him now in *England*, I with you could keep him
there) had the Impudence, some Years ago, in Parliament Time, to

---

* Supposed to be Mr. *Broderick*.

shake my Lord Bishop of *Killaloo* by his Lawn Sleeve, and tell him in a threatening Manner, *That he hoped to live to see the Day, when there should not be one of his Order in the Kingdom.*

These last Lines, perhaps, you think a Digression; therefore to return, I have told you the Consequences we fully reckon upon, from repealing the *Sacramental Test*, which although the greatest Number of such as are for doing it, are actually in no Manner of Pain about, and many of them care not three Pence whether there be any *Church* or no; yet, because they pretend to argue from Conscience as well as Policy and Interest, I thought it proper to understand and answer them accordingly.

Now, Sir, in Answer to your Question, Whether if any Attempt should be made here for repealing the *Sacramental Test*, it would be likely to succeed? The Number of profest *Dissenters* in this Parliament was, as I remember, something under a Dozen, and I cannot call to mind above Thirty others who were expected to fall in with them. This is certain, that the *Prebyterian* Party having with great Industry mustered up their Forces, did endeavour one Day, upon Occasion of a Hint in my Lord *Pembroke's* Speech, to introduce a Debate about repealing the *Test Clause*, when there appeared, at least, four to one Odds against them; and the ablest of those, who were reckoned the most stanch and thorough-paced *Whigs* upon all other Occasions, fell off with an Abhorence at the first Mention of this.

I must desire you to take Notice, that the Terms of *Whig* and *Tory*, do not properly express the different Interests in our Parliament. Whoever bears a true Veneration for the Glorious Memory of King *William*, as our great Deliverer from *Popery* and *Slavery*; whoever is firmly loyal to our present Queen, with an utter Abhorrence and Detestation of the *Pretender*; whoever approves the Succession to the Crown in the House of *Hanover*, and is for preserving the Doctrine and Discipline of the Church of *England*, with an *Indulgence* for scrupulous Consciences; such a Man, we think, acts upon right Principles, and may be justly allowed a *Whig*; and, I believe, there are not six Members in our House of Commons, who may not fairly come under this Description. So that the Parties among us are made up, on one side, of *moderate Whigs*, and, on the other, of *Presbyterians* and their *Abettors*; by which last I mean, such who can equally go to a *Church*, or a *Conventicle*; or such who are indifferent to all Religion in general; or, lastly, such who affect to bear a personal Rancor towards the Clergy. These last, are a Set of Men not of our own Growth; their Principles, at least, have been *imported* of late Years; yet this whole Party, put together, will not, I am confident, amount to above fifty Men in Parliament, which can hardly be worked up into a Majority of three Hundred.

As to the House of Lords, the Difficulty there is conceived, at least, as great as in ours. So many of our Temporal Peers live in *England*, that the Bishops are generally pretty near a *Par* of the House, and we reckon* they will be all to a Man against repealing the *Test*; and yet their Lordships are generally thought as good *Whigs* upon our Principles as any in the Kingdom. There are, indeed, a few Lay Lords who appear to have no great Devotion for *Episcopacy*; and perhaps one or two more, with whom *certain powerful Motives* might be used for removing any Difficulty whatsoever; but these are in no sort of a Number to carry any Point against a Conjunction of the rest, with the whole Bench of Bishops.

Besides, the intire Body of our Clergy is utterly against repealing the *Test*, although they are entirely devoted to her Majesty, and hardly One in a Hundred who are not very good *Whigs*, in our Acceptation of the Word. And I must let you know, that we of *Ireland*, are not yet come up to *other Folks Refinement*: For we generally love and esteem our Clergy, and think they deserve it; nay, we are apt to lay some Weight upon their Opinions, and would not willingly disoblige them, at least, unless it were upon some greater Point of Interest than this. And their Judgment, in the present Affair, is the more to be regarded, because they are the last Persons who will be affected by it: This makes us think them impartial, and that their Concern is only for Religion and the Interest of the Kingdom. Because, the Act which repeals the *Test*, will only qualify a *Layman* for an Employment, but not a *Presbyterian* or *Anabaptist* Preacher for a Church Living. Now I must take Leave to inform you, that several Members of our House, and my self among the rest, knowing, some Time ago, what was upon the Anvil, went to all the Clergy we knew of any Distinction, and desired their Judgment in the Matter, wherein we found a most wonderful Agreement; there being but *one Divine*, that we could hear of, in the whole Kingdom, who appeared of a contrary Sentiment; wherein he afterwards stood alone in the *Convocation*, very little to his *Credit*, although, as he hoped, very much to his *Interest*.

I will now consider, a little, the Arguments offered to shew the Advantages, or rather Necessity of repealing the *Test* in *Ireland*. We are told, the *Popish* Interest is here so formidable; that all Hands should be joined to keep it under; that the only Names of Distinctions among us, ought to be those of *Protestant* and *Papist*; and that this Expedient is the only Means to *unite* all Protestants

* N.B. Things are quite altered in that Bench, since this Discourse was written.

upon one common Bottom. All which is nothing but Misrepresentation and Mistake.

If we were under any real Fear of the *Papists* in this Kingdom, it would be hard to think us so stupid, as not to be equally apprehensive with *others*, since we are likely to be the greatest, and more immediate Sufferers; but, on the contrary, we look upon them to be altogether as inconsiderable as the Women and Children. Their Lands are almost entirely taken from them, and they are rendered uncapable of purchasing any more; and for the little that remains, Provision is made by the late Act against Popery, that it will daily crumble away: To prevent which, some of the most considerable among them are already turned Protestants, and so, in all Probability, will many more. Then, the Popish Priests are all registered, and without Permission (which, I hope, will not be granted) they can have no Successors; so that the Protestant Clergy will find it, perhaps, no difficult Matter to bring great Numbers over to the Church; and, in the mean Time, the common People without Leaders, without Discipline, or natural Courage, being little better than *Hewers of Wood, and Drawers of Water*, are out of all Capacity of doing any Mischief, if they were ever so well inclined. Neither are they, at all, likely to join in any considerable Numbers with an *Invader*, having found so ill Success when they were much more numerous and powerful; when they had a Prince of their own Religion to head them, had been trained for some Years under a *Popish Deputy*, and received such mighty Aids from the *French* King.

As to that Argument used for repealing the *Test*; that it will unite all Protestants against the *common Enemy*; I wonder by what Figure those Gentlemen speak, who are pleased to advance it: Suppose, on order to encrease the Friendship between you and me, a Law should pass that I must have Half your Estate; do you think that would much advance the Union between us? Or, suppose I share my Fortune equally between my own *Children*, and a *Stranger*, whom I take into my Protection; will that be a Method to unite them? It is an odd way of uniting Parties, to deprive a *Majority* of Part of their antient Right, by conferring it on a *Faction* who had never any Right at all, and therefore cannot be said to suffer any Loss or Injury, if it be refused them. Neither is it very clear, how far some People may stretch the Term of *common Enemy*: How many are there of those that call themselves Protestants, who look upon our Worship to be idolatrous as well as that of the *Papists*, and with great Charity put *Prelacy* and *Popery* together, as Terms convertible?

And, therefore, there is one small Doubt I would be willingly satisfied in, before I agree to the repealing of the *Test*; that is, whether these same Protestants, when they have, by their Dexterity, made themselves the National Religion, and disposed the Church Revenues among their *Pastors* or *Themselves*, will be so kind to allow *us Dissenters*, I do not say a Share in Employments, but a bare *Toleration* by Law. The Reason of my Doubt is, because I have been so very idle as to read above fifty Pamphlets, written by as many *Presbyterian* Divines, loudly disclaiming this Idol *Toleration*; some of them calling it (I know not how properly) a *Rag of Popery*, and all agreeing, it was to *establish Iniquity by a Law*. Now, I would be glad to know when and where *their Successors* have renounced this Doctrine, and before what Witnesses. Because, methinks, I should be loath to see my poor titular Bishop *in partibus*, seized on by Mistake in the Dark for a Jesuit, or be forced my self to keep a Chaplain disguised like my Butler, and steal to Prayers in a back Room, as my Grandfather used in those Times when the Church of *England* was *malignant*.[5]

But this is ripping up old Quarrels long forgot: *Popery* is now the *common Enemy*, against which we must all unite: I have been tired in History with the perpetual Folly of those States, who called in Foreigners to assist them against a *common Enemy*: But the Mischief was, these *Allies* would never be brought to allow that the *common Enemy* was quite subdued. And they had Reason; for it proved at last, that one Part of the *common Enemy* was those who called them in; and so the *Allies* became at length the *Masters*.

It is agreed, among Naturalists, that a *Lyon* is a larger, a stronger, and more dangerous Enemy than a *Cat*; yet if a Man were to have his Choice, either a *Lyon* at his Foot, bound fast with three or four Chains, his Teeth drawn out, and his Claws pared to the Quick, or an angry *Cat* in full Liberty at his Throat; he would take no long Time to determine.

I have been sometimes admiring the wonderful Significancy of that Word *Persecution*, and what various Interpretations it hath acquired even within my Memory. When I was a Boy, I often heard the *Presbyterians* complain, that they were not permitted to serve God in their own Way; they said, they did not repine at our Employments, but thought that all Men, who live peaceably, ought to have Liberty of Conscience, and Leave to assemble. That Impediment being removed at the Revolution, they soon learned to swallow the *Sacramental Test*, and began to take very large Steps, wherein all

5 Thomas Swift, vicar of Goodrich, Herefordshire. Swift revered the memory of his paternal grandfather for active loyalty to King Charles and his fierce hostility to the Cromwellians. See Swift's autobiographical essay, *Family of Swift*, in *Prose Works* V, pp. 187–195.

who offered to oppose them, were called Men of a *persecuting Spirit*. During the Time the Bill against Occasional Conformity was on Foot, *Persecution* was every Day rung in our Ears, and now at last the *Sacramental Test* it self has the same Name. Where then is this Matter likely to end, when the obtaining of one Request is only used as a Step to demand another? A Lover is ever complaining of *Cruelty*, while any thing is denied him; and when the Lady ceases to be *cruel*, she is from the next Moment at his Mercy: So *Persecution*, it seems, is every Thing that will not leave it in Men's Power to *persecute others*.

There is one Argument offered against a *Sacramental Test*, by a Sort of Men who are content to be stiled of the Church of *England*, who, perhaps, attend its Service in the Morning, and go with their Wives to a *Conventicle* in the Afternoon, confessing they hear very good Doctrine in both. These Men are much offended, that so holy an Institution as that of the Lord's Supper, should be made subservient to such mercenary Purposes, as the getting of an Employment. Now, it seems, the Law concluding all Men to be Members of that Church where they receive the Sacrament; and supposing all Men to live like Christians (especially those who are to have Employments) did imagine they received the Sacrament, in Course, about four Times a Year, and therefore only desired it might appear by Certificate to the Publick, that such who took an Office, were Members of the Church established, by doing their ordinary Duty. However, *lest we should offend them*, we have often desired they would deal candidly with us; for if the Matter stuck only there, we would propose it in Parliament, that every Man who takes an Employment, should, instead of receiving the Sacrament, be obliged to swear, that he is a member of the Church of *Ireland* by Law established, with *Episcopacy, and so forth*; and as they do now in *Scotland, to be true to the Kirk*. But when we drive them thus far, they always retire to the main Body of the Argument, urge the Hardship that Men should be deprived the Liberty of serving their Queen and Country, on Account of their Conscience: And, in short, have Recourse to the common Stile of their half Brethren. Now, whether this be a sincere Way of arguing, I will appeal to any other Judgment but theirs.

There is another Topick of Clamour somewhat parallel to the foregoing; it seems, by the Test Clause, the *Military* Officers are obliged to receive the Sacrament as well as the *Civil*. And it is a Matter of some Patience, to hear the *Dissenters* declaiming upon this Occasion: They cry they are *disarmed*, they are used like *Papists*; when an Enemy appears at Home, or from Abroad, they must sit still, and see their Throats cut, or be hanged for High Treason if they offer to defend themselves. Miserable Condition! Woeful Dilemma! It is happy for us all, that the Pretender was not apprised of this *passive Presbyterian* Principle, else he would have infallibly landed in our *Northern Parts*, and found them all sat down in their Formalities, as the *Gauls* did the *Roman* Senators, ready to die with Honour in their Callings. Sometimes, to appease their Indignation, we venture to give them Hopes, that, in such a Case, the Government will perhaps connive, and hardly be so severe to hang them for defending it against the Letter of the Law; to which they readily answer, that they will not lie at our Mercy, but let us fight our Battles our selves. Sometimes we offer to get an Act, by which, upon all *Popish* Insurrections at Home, or *Popish* Invasions from Abroad, the Government shall be impowered to grant Commissions to all Protestants whatsoever, without that *persecuting* Circumstance of obliging them to *say their Prayers* when they receive the Sacrament; but they abhor all Thoughts of *occasional* Commissions, they will not do our Drudgery, and we reap the Benefit; it is not worth their while to fight *pro Aris & focis;*[6] and they had rather lose their Estates, Liberties, Religion and Lives, than the Pleasure of *governing.*

But to bring this Discourse towards a Conclusion. If the Dissenters will be satisfied with such a *Toleration* by Law, as hath been granted them in *England,* I believe the Majority of both Houses will fall readily in with it; farther it will be hard to perswade this House of Commons, and, perhaps, much harder the next. For, to say the Truth, we make a mighty Difference here between suffering *Thistles* to grow among us, and wearing them for *Posies.* We are fully convinced in our Consciences, that *We* shall always *tolerate them,* but not quite so fully, that *They* will always *tolerate us,* when it comes to their Turn; and *We* are the Majority, and *We* are in Possession.

He who argues in Defence of a Law in Force, not antiquated or obsolete, but lately enacted, is certainly on the safer Side, and may be allowed to point out the Dangers he conceives to foresee in the Abrogation of it.

For if the Consequences of repealing this Clause, should, at some time or other, enable the *Presbyterians* to work themselves up into the National Church; instead of *uniting* Protestants, it would sow eternal Divisions among them. First, their own Sects which now lie dormant, would be soon at Cuffs *again* with each other, about Power and Preferment; and the *Dissenting Episcopals,* perhaps, discontented to such a Degree, as, upon some *fair unhappy* Occasion, would be able to shake the firmest Loyalty, which none can deny theirs to be.

6 For Hearth and Home. Latin proverb.

Neither is it very difficult to conjecture, from some late Proceedings, at what a Rate this *Faction* is like to drive wherever it gets the *Whip* and the *Seat*. They have already set up Courts of Spiritual Judicature, in open Contempt of the Law: They send *Missionaries* every where, without being invited, in order to *convert* the Church of *England* Folks to *Christianity*. They are as vigilant as *I know who*, to attend Persons on their Death-Beds, and for Purposes much alike. And what Practices such Principles as these (with many others that might be invidious to mention) may spawn, when they are *laid out to the Sun*, you may determine at Leisure.

Lastly, whether we are so entirely sure of their Loyalty upon the present Foot of Government as you may imagine, their Detractors make a Question, which, however, does, I think, by no Means affect the Body of *Dissenters*; but the Instance produced, is of some among their leading Teachers in the *North*, who refused the *Abjuration Oath*, yet continue their Preaching, and have Abundance of Followers. The Particulars are out of my Head, but the Fact is notorious enough, and, I believe, hath been published; I think it a Pity it has not been *remedied*.

Thus I have fairly given you, Sir, my own Opinion, as well as that of a great Majority in both Houses here, relating to this weighty Affair, upon which, I am confident, you may securely reckon. I will leave you to make what Use of it you please.

A
PROPOSAL

FOR THE

UNIVERSAL USE

OF

Irish Manufacture,

IN

Cloaths, and Furniture of Houses, *&c.*

UTTERLY

Rejecting and *Renouncing* every Thing
wearable that comes from
ENGLAND.

Written in the Year 1720

This *Proposal*, which appeared anonymously in May 1720, was Swift's first Irish pamphlet after his appointment, in 1713, as Dean of St. Patrick's. To maximise its effect, it was deliberately timed to coincide with celebrations of King George's sixtieth birthday. Partly motivated by defence of the weaving-trade in his own parish, Swift's defiant political justification for an economic boycott caused a legal uproar. The printer was taken to court, but the jury refused to find either him or the pamphlet guilty of an offence. A year later, the case was dropped, by an order of *noli prosequi* from the incoming Lord Lieutenant, the Duke of Grafton. Swift never forgot or forgave this attempt at legal censorship.

A
PROPOSAL

FOR THE

UNIVERSAL USE
OF
Irish MANUFACTURE, &c.

IT is the peculiar Felicity and Prudence of the People in this
Kingdom, that whatever Commodities, or Productions, lie under the
greatest Discouragements from *England*, those are what they are sure
to be most industrious in cultivating and spreading. *Agriculture*,
which hath been the principal Care of all wise Nations, and for the
Encouragement whereof there are so many Statute-Laws in *England*,
we countenance so well, that the Landlords are every where, by *penal
Clauses*, absolutely prohibiting their Tenants from Plowing; not
satisfied to confine them within certain Limitations, as it is the Practice of the *English*; one Effect of which, is already seen in the prodigious Dearness of Corn, and the Importation of it from *London*,
as the cheaper market: And, because People are the *Riches of a Country*,[1] and that our *Neighbours* have done, and are doing all that in
them lie, to make our Wool a Drug to us, and a Monopoly to them;
therefore, the Politick Gentlemen of *Ireland* have depopulated vasts
Tracts of the best Land, for the feeding of Sheep.

I could fill a Volume as large as the *History of the wise Men of
Goatham*, with a Catalogue only of some *wonderful* Laws and
Customs we have observed within thirty Years past. It is true, indeed,
our beneficial Traffick of Wool with *France*, hath been our only Support for several Years past; furnishing us all the little Money we have
to pay our Rents, and go to Market. But our Merchants assure me, *This
Trade hath received a great Damp by the present fluctuating Condition of the Coin in France; and that most of their Wine is paid for in
Specie, without carrying thither any Commodity from hence.*

---

1 Conventional mercantilist wisdom of the period. Swift repeatedly showed how
  Ireland's case contradicted such a proposition.

However, since we are so universally bent upon enlarging our *Flocks*, it may be worth inquiring, what we shall do with our Wool, in case *Barnstable* should be over-stocked, and our *French* Commerce should fail?

I should wish the Parliament had thought fit to have suspended their Regulation of *Church* Matters, and Enlargements of the *Prerogative*, until a more convenient Time, because they did not appear very pressing, (at least to the Persons *principally concerned*) and, instead of those great Refinements in *Politicks* and *Divinity*, had *amused* Themselves and their Committees, a little, with the *State of the Nation*. For Example: What if the House of Commons had thought fit to make a Resolution, *Nemine Contradicente*, against wearing any Cloath or Stuff in their Families, which were not of the Growth and Manufacture of this Kingdom? What if they had extended it so far, as utterly to exclude all Silks, Velvets, Calicoes, and the whole *Lexicon* of Female Fopperies; and declared, that whoever acted otherwise, should be deemed and reputed *an Enemy to the Nation*? What if they had sent up such a Resolution to be agreed to by the House of Lords; and by their own Practice and En-couragement, spread the Execution of it in their several Countries? What if we should agree to make *burying in Woollen a Fashion*, as our Neighbours have made it a *Law*? What if the Ladies would be content with *Irish* Stuffs for the Furniture of their Houses, for Gowns and Petticoats to themselves and their Daughters? Upon the whole, and to crown all the rest, let a firm Resolution be taken, by *Male* and *Female*, never to appear with one single *Shred* that comes from *England; and let all the People say*, AMEN.

I hope, and believe, nothing could please his Majesty better than to hear that his loyal Subjects, of both Sexes, in this Kingdom, celebrated his *Birth-Day* (now approaching) *universally* clad in their own Manufacture. Is there Vertue enough left in this deluded People to save them from the Brink of Ruin? If the Mens Opinions may be taken, the Ladies will look as handsome in Stuffs as Brocades, and, since all will be equal, there may be room enough to employ their Wit and Fancy in chusing and matching of Patterns and Colours. I heard the late Archbishop of *Tuam* mention a pleasant Observation of some Body's; *that* Ireland *would never be happy 'till a Law were made for* burning *every* Thing *that came from* England, *except their* People *and their* Coals: I must confess, that as to the former, I should not be sorry if they would stay at home; and for the latter, I hope, in a little Time we shall have no Occasion for them.

Non tanti mitra est, non tanti Judicis ostrum.[2]

2 A mitre is not worth so much, a judge's purple is not worth so much.

But I should rejoice to see a *Stay-Lace* from *England* be thought *scandalous*, and become a Topick for *Censure* at *Visits* and *Tea Tables*.

If the unthinking Shopkeepers in this Town, had not been *utterly* destitute of common Sense, they would have made some *Proposal to the Parliament*, with a *Petition* to the Purpose I have mentioned; promising to improve the *Cloaths and Stuffs of the Nation, into all possible Degrees of Fineness and Colours, and engaging not to play the Knave, according to their Custom, by exacting and imposing upon the Nobility and Gentry, either as to the Prices or the Goodness.* For I remember, in *London*, upon a general Mourning, the *rascally Mercers* and *Woollen Drapers*, would, in Four and Twenty Hours, raise their *Cloaths* and *Silks* to above a double Price; and if the Mourning continued long, then come whingeing with *Petitions* to the *Court, that they were ready to starve, and their Fineries lay upon their Hands.*

I could wish our Shopkeepers would immediately think on this *Proposal*, addressing it to all Persons of Quality, and others; but first be sure to get some Body who can write Sense, to put it into Form.

I think it needless to exhort the *Clergy* to follow this good Example, because, *in a little Time, those among them who are so unfortunate to have had their Birth and Education in this Country, will think themselves abundantly happy when they can afford* Irish *Crape, and an* Athlone *Hat*; and as to the others, I *shall not presume* to direct them. I have, indeed, seen the present Archbishop of *Dublin* clad from Head to Foot in our own Manufacture; and yet, under the Rose be it spoken, *his Grace deserves as good a Gown, as if he had not been born among us.*

I have not Courage enough to offer *one Syllable* on this Subject to *their Honours* of the Army: Neither have I sufficiently considered the great Importance of *Scarlet* and *Gold Lace.*

The Fable, in *Ovid*, of *Arachne* and *Pallas*, is to this Purpose. The Goddess had heard of one *Arachne* a young Virgin, very famous for *Spinning* and *Weaving*: They both met upon a Tryal of Skill; and *Pallas* finding herself almost equalled in her own Art, stung with Rage and Envy, knockt her *Rival* down, turned her into a *Spyder*, enjoining her to *spin* and *weave* for ever, *out of her own Bowels*, and *in a very narrow Compass*. I confess, that from a Boy, I always pitied poor *Arachne*, and could never heartily love the Goddess, on Account of so *cruel and unjust a Sentence*; which, however, is *fully executed* upon *Us* by *England*, with further Additions of *Rigor* and *Severity*. For the greatest Part of *our Bowels and Vitals* is extracted, without allowing us the Liberty of *spinning* and *weaving* them.

The Scripture tells us, that *Oppression makes a wise Man mad*; therefore, consequently speaking, the Reason why some Men are not *mad*, is because they are not *wise*: However, it were to be wished that *Oppression* would, in Time, teach a little *Wisdom* to *Fools*.

I was much delighted with a Person, who hath a great Estate in this Kingdom, upon his Complaints to me, *how grievously POOR* England *suffers by Impositions from* Ireland. *That we convey our own Wool to* France, *in Spight of all the* Harpies *at the Custom-House. That Mr.* Shutleworth, *and others on the* Cheshire *Coasts, are such Fools to sell us their Bark at a good Price, for tanning our own Hydes into Leather; with other Enormities of the like Weight and Kind.* To which I will venture to add more: *That the Mayorality of this City is always executed by an* Inhabitant, *and often by a* Native, *which might as well be done by a* Deputy, *with a moderate Salary, whereby POOR* England *loseth, at least, one thousand Pounds a Year upon the Ballance. That the Governing of this Kingdom costs the Lord Lieutenant three Thousand six Hundred Pounds a Year, so much net Loss to POOR* England. *That the People of* Ireland *presume to dig for Coals in their own Grounds; and the Farmers in the County of* Wicklow *send their Turf to the very Market of* Dublin, *to the great Discouragement of the Coal Trade at* Mostyn *and* White-haven. *That the Revenues of the Post Office here, so righteously belonging to the* English *Treasury, as arising chiefly from our own Commerce with each other, should be remitted to* London, *clogged with that grievous Burthen of Exchange, and the Pensions paid out of the* Irish *Revenues to* English *Favourites, should lie under the same Disadvantage, to the great Loss of the Grantees. When a* Divine *is sent over to a Bishoprick here, with the Hopes of Five and Twenty Hundred Pounds a Year; upon his Arrival, he finds, alas! a dreadful Discount of Ten or Twelve per Cent. A* Judge, *or a* Commissioner *of the Revenue, has the same Cause of Complaint.* Lastly, *The Ballad upon* Cotter *is vehemently suspected to be* Irish *Manufacture; and yet is allowed to be sung in our open Streets, under the very* Nose *of the* Government.[3]

These are a *few* among the many Hardships we put upon that *POOR* Kingdom of *England*; for which, I am confident, every *honest* Man wisheth a *Remedy*: And, I hear, there is a Project *on Foot* for transporting our best Wheaten *Straw*, by Sea and Land Carriage, to *Dunstable*; and *obliging us by a Law*, to take off yearly so many *Tun of Straw-Hats*, for the Use of our Women; which will be a

3 Sir James Cotter, prominent Catholic of Co. Cork, executed on 7 May, 1720, for rape. His trial aroused great public interest and controversy.

great Encouragement to the Manufacture of that *industrious* Town. I would be glad to learn among the Divines, whether a Law *to bind Men without their own Consent*, be obligatory *in foro Conscientiae*; because, I find *Scripture, Sanderson and Suarez*,[4] are wholly silent in the Matter. The Oracle of *Reason*, the great *Law of Nature*, and general Opinion of *Civilians*, wherever they treat of *limitted Governments*, are, indeed, decisive enough.

It is wonderful to observe the Biass among our People in favour of *Things, Persons*, and *Wares* of all Kinds that come from *England*. The *Printer* tells his *Hawkers*, that *he has got an excellent new Song just brought from* London. I have somewhat of a Tendency that way my self; and upon hearing a *Coxcomb* from thence displaying himself, with great Volubility, upon the *Park*, the *Play-House*, the *Opera*, the *Gaming Ordinaries*, it was apt to beget in me a Kind of Veneration for his Parts and Accomplishments. It is not many Years, since I remember a *Person* who, by his Style and Literature, seems to have been *Corrector* of a Hedge Press, in some *Blind-Alley* about *Little-Britain*, proceed *gradually* to be an *Author*, at least a * *Translator* of a lower Rate, although somewhat of a larger Bulk, than any that now *flourishes* in *Grub-street*; and, upon the Strength of this Foundation, came over *here; erect* himself up into an *Orator* and *Politician*, and lead a *Kingdom* after him. This, I am told, was the *very Motive* that prevailed on the ** *Author* of a Play called, *Love in a Hollow-Tree*, to do us the *Honour* of a Visit; presuming, with very good Reason, *that he was a Writer of a superior Class*. I know *another*, who, for thirty Years past, hath been the *common Standard of Stupidity in England*, where he was never heard a Minute in any *Assembly*, or by any *Party*, with *common Christian Treatment*; yet, upon his Arrival hither, could put on a *Face of Importance and Authority*, talked more than Six, without either *Gracefulness, Propriety*, or *Meaning*; and, at the same Time, be admired and followed as the Pattern of *Eloquence* and *Wisdom*.

Nothing hath humbled me so much, or shewn a greater Disposition to a *contemptuous* Treatment of *Ireland* in some chief *Governors*, than that high Style of several Speeches from the *Throne*, delivered, as usual, after the *Royal Assent*, in *some Periods* of the two last *Reigns*. Such Exaggerations of the prodigious

---

* Supposed to be *Caesar's* Commentaries, dedicated to the D[*uke*] of *Marlborough*.
**L. G. [*ri*] mst [*a*] n.
4 Robert Sanderson (1660–1741). Historian and archivist of common-law. In 1715 he applied unsuccessfully, (like Swift), for post of Royal Historiographer. Francisco de Suarez, Spanish Jesuit and scholastic philosopher. Wrote *Defensio Fidei* (1613), criticising divine right theories of James I.

Condescensions in the Prince, to pass *those good Laws*, would have
but an odd Sound at *Westminster:* Neither do I apprehend, how any
good Law can pass, wherein the *King's* Interest is not as much concerned as that of the *People*. I remember, after a Speech on the like
Occasion, delivered by my Lord *Wharton*.[5] (I think it was his last)
he desired Mr. *Addison to ask my Opinion of it:* My Answer was,
*That his Excellency had very honestly forfeited his Head, on
Account of one Paragraph; wherein he asserted, by plain Consequence*, a dispensing Power *in the Queen*. His Lordship owned *it was
true*, but *swore* the Words were *put into his Mouth* by direct Orders
from Court. From whence it is clear, that some *Ministers* in those
Times, were apt, from their *high* Elevation, to look *down* upon this
Kingdom, as if it had been one of their *Colonies* of *Out-casts* in
America. And I observed a little of the same Turn of Spirit in *some great
Men*, from whom I expected better; although, to do them Justice, it
proved no Point of Difficulty to make them *correct their Idea*, whereof
the *whole Nation* quickly found the Benefit. — But that is *forgotten*.
How the Style hath since run, I am wholly a Stranger; having never
seen a Speech since the last of the Queen.

I would now expostulate a little with our Country Landlords; who,
by unmeasurable *screwing* and *racking* their Tenants all over the
Kingdom, have already reduced the miserable *People* to a *worse Condition* than the *Peasants* in *France*, or the *Vassals* in *Germany* and
Poland; so that the whole *Species* of what we call *Substantial
Farmers*, will, in a very few Years, be utterly at an End. It was pleasant to observe these Gentlemen, *labouring* with all their *Might*, for
preventing the *Bishops* from letting their Revenues at a moderate
half Value, (whereby the whole *Order* would, in an Age, have been
reduced to manifest Beggary) at the very Instant, when they were
every where *canting* their own Lands upon short Leases, and sacrificing their *oldest Tenants for a Penny an Acre advance*. I know not
how it comes to pass, (and yet, perhaps, I know well enough) that
Slaves have a natural Disposition to be *Tyrants*; and that when my
Betters give me a Kick, I am apt to revenge it with six upon my *Footman*; although, perhaps, he may be an honest and diligent Fellow.
I have heard *great* Divines affirm, that *nothing is so likely to call
down an universal Judgment from Heaven upon a Nation, as universal Oppression*; and whether this be not already verified in Part, *their
Worships* the Landlords are *now* at full Leisure to consider. Whoever
travels this Country, and observes the *Face* of Nature, or the *Faces*,

5 Thomas Wharton (1648–1715). Leading Whig politician loathed by Swift. Lord
   Lieutenant of Ireland, 1708–10, with Joseph Addison, poet and friend of Swift,
   as his Secretary.

and Habits, and Dwellings of the *Natives*, will hardly think himself in a Land where either *Law, Religion,* or common *Humanity* is professed.

I CANNOT forbear saying one Word upon a *Thing* they call a *Bank*, which, I hear, is projecting in this Town.[6] I never saw the *Proposals*, nor understand any one Particular of their Scheme: What I wish for, at present, is only a sufficient provision of *Hemp*, and *Caps*, and *Bells*, to distribute according to the several Degrees of *Honesty* and *Prudence* in *some Persons*. I *hear* only of a monstrous Sum already named; and, if OTHERS do not soon hear of it too, and *hear* it with a Vengeance, then am I a Gentleman of less Sagacity than my self, and very few besides, take me to be. And the Jest will be still the better, if it be true, as judicious Persons have assured me, that one Half of this Money will be *real*, and the other Half altogether imaginary. The Matter will be likewise much mended, if the Merchants continue to carry off our Gold, and our Goldsmiths to melt down our heavy Silver.

6 An afterthought. Swift wrote several other pamphlets opposing the idea of a National Bank. See *Prose Works* IX, pp. 281–310.

A
LETTER

TO THE

Shop-Keepers, Tradesmen, Farmers,

AND

Common-People of *Ireland,*

CONCERNING THE

BRASS HALF-PENCE

Coined by one *WILLIAM WOOD,*
Hard-Ware-Man,

With a DESIGN to have them pass in this
KINGDOM.

Wherein is shewn,

The Power of his PATENT, the Value of the HALF-PENCE, and how far every Person may be obliged to take the same in Payments, and how to behave himself, in Case such an Attempt should be made by WOOD, or any other Person.

(Very proper to be kept in every FAMILY.)

By *M. B.* DRAPIER.

Written in the YEAR 1724

This is the opening polemic of *The Drapier's Letters*, a series of seven pamphlets written in 1724 and early 1725, to arouse public opposition to Wood's patent and the arbitrary rule which permitted it. Money was always one of Swift's favourite topics. The mask of a simple tradesman, standing forth as Ireland's David to England's Goliath, led to the greatest triumph in Swift's Irish career. The government was forced to revoke the patent, and the Dean was forever hailed as the 'Hibernian Patriot'. The political rhetoric of the *Letters* is a landmark in eighteenth-century Irish history.

A
LETTER

To the *Tradesmen, Shop-Keepers, Farmers,* and *Country-People* in General, of the Kingdom of *Ireland.*

Brethren, Friends, Countrymen, and *Fellow Subjects.*

WHAT I intend now to say to you, is, next to your Duty to God, and the Care of your Salvation, of the greatest Concern to your selves, and your Children; your *Bread* and *Cloathing*, and every common Necessary of Life entirely depend upon it. Therefore I do most earnestly exhort you as *Men*, as *Christians*, as *Parents*, and as *Lovers of your Country*, to read this Paper with the utmost Attention, or get it read to you by others; which that you may do at the less Expence, I have ordered the Printer to sell it at the lowest Rate.

It is a great Fault among you, that when a Person writes with no other Intention than *to do you Good, you will not be at the Pains to read his Advices:* One Copy of this Paper may serve a Dozen of you, which will be less than a Farthing a-piece. It is your Folly, that you have no common or general Interest in your View, not even the Wisest among you; neither do you know or enquire, or care who are your Friends, or who are your Enemies.

About four Years ago, a little Book was written to advise all People to wear the * *Manufactures of this our own Dear Country:* It had no other Design, said nothing against the *King* or *Parliament*, or *any* Person whatsoever, yet the POOR PRINTER was prosecuted two Years, with the utmost Violence; and even some WEAVERS themselves, for whose Sake it was written, being upon the JURY, FOUND HIM GUILTY. This would be enough to discourage any Man from endeavouring to do you Good, when you will either neglect

---

* Vide *one of the preceding Pamphlets, entitled, A Proposal for the Use of Irish Manufactures.*

him, or fly in his Face for his Pains; and when he must expect only *Danger to himself*, and to be fined and imprisoned, perhaps to his Ruin.

However, I cannot but warn you once more of the manifest Destruction before your Eyes, if you do not behave your selves as you ought.

I will therefore first tell you the *plain Story of the Fact*; and then I will lay before you, how you ought to act in common Prudence, and according to the *Laws of your Country*.

The Fact is thus; It having been many Years since COPPER HALF-PENCE or FARTHINGS were last Coined in this *Kingdom*, they have been for some Time very scarce, and many *Counterfeits* passed about under the Name of RAPS: Several Applications were made to *England*, that we might have Liberty to *Coin New Ones*, as in former Times we did; but they did not succeed. At last one Mr. WOOD, *a mean ordinary Man, a Hard-Ware Dealer*, procured a *Patent* under His MAJESTY'S BROAD SEAL, to coin 108000 *l.* in *Copper* for this *Kingdom*; which Patent however did not oblige any one here to take them, unless they pleased. Now you must know, that the HALF-PENCE and FARTHINGS in *England* pass for very little more than they are worth: And if you should beat them to Pieces, and sell them to the *Brazier*, you would not lose much above a Penny in a Shilling. But Mr. WOOD made his HALF-PENCE of such *Base Metal*, and so much smaller than the *English* ones, that the *Brazier* would hardly give you above a *Penny* of good Money for a *Shilling* of his; so that this Sum of 108000 *l.* in good Gold and Silver, must be given for TRASH that will not be worth above *Eight or Nine Thousand Pounds* real Value. But this is not the Worst; for Mr. WOOD, when he pleases, may by Stealth send over *another 108000 l.* and buy *all our Goods for Eleven Parts in Twelve*, under the Value. For Example, if a *Hatter* sells a Dozen of *Hats* for Five Shillings a-piece, which amounts to *Three Pounds*, and receives the Payment in Mr. WOOD'S Coin, he really receives only the Value of *Five Shillings*.

Perhaps you will wonder how such *an ordinary Fellow* as this Mr. WOOD could have so much Interest as to get HIS MAJESTY'S Broad Seal for so great a Sum of bad Money,[1] to be sent to this poor Country; and that all the *Nobility* and *Gentry* here could not obtain the same Favour, and let us make our own HALF-PENCE, as we used to do. Now I will make that Matter very plain. We are at a great Distance from the *King's Court*, and have no body there to solicit for us, although a great Number of *Lords* and *Squires*,

1 There was a widespread story that Wood had obtained the patent through a bribe to the King's mistress, the Duchess of Kendal.

whose Estates are here, and are our Countrymen, spend all their *Lives* and *Fortunes* there. But this same Mr. WOOD was able to attend constantly for his own Interest; he is an ENGLISHMAN and had GREAT FRIENDS, and it seems knew very well *where to give Money*, to those that would speak to OTHERS that could speak to the KING, and would tell a FAIR STORY. And HIS MAJESTY, and perhaps the great Lord or Lords who advised him, might think it was for our *Country's Good*, and so, as the Lawyers express it, the KING was deceived in his Grant; which often happens in *all Reigns*. And I am sure if HIS MAJESTY knew that such a Patent, if it should take Effect according to the Desire of Mr. WOOD, would utterly ruin this Kingdom, which hath given such great Proofs of its *Loyalty*; he would immediately recall it, and perhaps shew his Displeasure to SOME BODY OR OTHER : *But a Word to the Wise is enough.* Most of you must have heard with what Anger our *Honourable House of Commons* received an Account of this WOOD'S PATENT. There were several *Fine Speeches* made upon it, and plain Proofs, that it was all a WICKED CHEAT from the *Bottom to the Top*; and several *smart Votes* were printed, which that same WOOD had the Assurance to answer likewise in *Print*, and in so confident a Way, as if he were *a better Man than our whole Parliament* put together.

   This WOOD, as soon as his *Patent* was passed, or soon after, sends over a great many *Barrels of those* HALF-PENCE, to *Cork* and other *Sea Port Towns*, and to get them off, offered an *Hundred Pounds* in his *Coin* for *Seventy* or *Eighty* in *Silver:* But the *Collectors* of the KING'S Customs very honestly refused to take them, and so did almost every body else. And since the Parliament hath condemned them, and desired the KING that they might be stopped, all the *Kingdom* do abominate them.

   But WOOD is still working *under hand* to force his HALF-PENCE upon us; and if he can by help of his *Friends* in *England* prevail so far as to get an Order that the *Commissioners* and *Collectors* of the *King's* Money shall receive them, and that the *Army* is to be paid with them, then he thinks *his Work shall be done.* And this is the Difficulty you will be under in such a *Case:* For the common Soldier when he goes to the *Market* or *Ale-house*, will offer this Money, and if it be refused, perhaps he will *swagger* and *hector*, and *threaten* to *beat the Butcher* or *Ale wife*, or take the Goods by Force, and throw them the bad HALF-PENCE. In this and the like Cases, the *Shop-keeper*, or *Victualler*, or *any other Tradesman* has no more to do, than to demand ten times the Price of his Goods, if it is to be paid in WOOD'S Money; for Example, Twenty Pence of that Money for a *Quart of Ale*, and so in all things else, and not part with his Goods till he gets the *Money*.

For suppose you go to an *Ale-house* with that base Money, and the *Landlord* gives you a Quart for Four or these HALF-PENCE, what must the *Victualler* do? His *Brewer* will not be paid in that Coin, or if the *Brewer* should be such a Fool, the *Farmers* will not take it from them for their *Bere, because they are bound by their Leases to pay their Rents in Good and Lawful Money of *England*, which this is not, nor of *Ireland* neither, and the *Squire their Landlord* will never be so bewitched to take such *Trash* for his Land; so that it must certainly stop somewhere or other, and wherever it stops it is the same Thing, and we are all undone.

The common Weight of those HALF-PENCE is between four and five to an *Ounce*; suppose five, then three Shillings and four Pence will weigh a Pound, and consequently *Twenty Shillings* will weigh *Six Pounds Butter Weight*. Now there are many hundred *Farmers* who pay Two Hundred Pounds a Year Rent: Therefore when one of these *Farmers* comes with his Half-Year's Rent, which is One Hundred Pound, it will be at least Six hundred Pound weight, which is Three Horses Load.

If a *Squire* has a mind to come to Town to buy Cloaths and Wine and Spices for himself and Family, or perhaps to pass the Winter here, he must bring with him five or six Horses loaden with *Sacks* as the *Farmers* bring their Corn; and when his Lady comes in her Coach to our Shops, it must be followed by a Car loaded with Mr. WOOD'S Money. And I hope we shall have the Grace to take it for no more than it is worth.

They say SQUIRE CONOLLY has *Sixteen Thousand Pounds a Year;*[2] now if he sends for his *Rent* to Town, *as it is likely he does*, he must have *Two Hundred and Fifty Horses* to bring up his *Half Year's Rent*, and two or three great *Cellars* in his House for Stowage. But what the Bankers will do I cannot tell. For I am assured, that some great Bankers keep by them *Forty Thousand Pounds* in ready Cash to answer all Payments, which Sum in Mr. WOOD'S Money, would require Twelve Hundred Horses to carry it.

For my own Part, I am already resolved what to do; I have a pretty good Shop of *Irish Stuffs* and *Silks*, and instead of taking Mr. WOOD'S bad Copper, I intend to Truck with my Neighbours the *Butchers*, and *Bakers*, and *Brewers*, and the rest, *Goods for Goods*, and the little *Gold* and *Silver* I have, I will keep by me like my *Heart's Blood* till better Times, or until I am just ready to starve, and then I will buy Mr. WOOD'S Money, as my Father did the Brass Money

---

* *A sort of Barley in* Ireland.
2 William Conolly (1660–1729). Lord Justice of Ireland, and Speaker of the Irish House of Commons. Reputedly one of the wealthiest men in Ireland.

in King *James's* Time; who could buy *Ten Pound* of it with a *Guinea*, and I hope to get as much for a *Pistole*, and so purchase *Bread* from those who will be such Fools as to sell it me.

These *Half-pence*, if they once pass, will soon be *Counterfeit*, because it may be cheaply done, the *Stuff* is so *Base*. The *Dutch* likewise will probably do the same thing, and send them over to us to pay for our *Goods*; and Mr. WOOD will never be at rest, but coin on: So that in some Years we shall have at least five Times 108000 *l.* of this *Lumber*. Now the current Money of this Kingdom is not reckoned to be above Four Hundred Thousand Pounds in all; and while there is a *Silver* Six-Pence left, these *Blood suckers* will never be quiet.

When once the *Kingdom* is reduced to such a Condition, I will tell you what must be the End: The *Gentlemen of Estates* will all turn off their *Tenants* for want of Payment; because, as I told you before, the *Tenants* are obliged by their Leases to pay *Sterling*, which is Lawful Current Money of *England*; then they will turn their own *Farmers*, *as too many of them do already*, run *all* into *Sheep* where they can, keeping only such other *Cattle* as are necessary; then they will be their own *Merchants*, and send their *Wool*, and *Butter*, and *Hides*, and *Linnen* beyond Sea for ready *Money*, and *Wine*, and *Spices*, and *Silks*. They will keep only a few miserable *Cottagers*. The *Farmers* must *Rob* or *Beg*, or leave their *Countrey*. The *Shopkeepers* in this and every other Town, must *Break* and *Starve:* For it is the *Landed-man* that maintains the *Merchant*, and *Shop-keeper*, and *Handicrafts-Man*.

But when the *Squire* turns *Farmer* and *Merchant* himself, all the good Money he gets from abroad, he will hoard up to send for *England*, and keep some poor *Taylor* or *Weaver*, and the like, in his own House, who will be glad to get Bread at any Rate.

I should never have done, if I were to tell you all the Miseries that we shall undergo, if we be so *Foolish* and *Wicked* as to take this *Cursed Coin*. It would be very hard, if all *Ireland* should be put into *One Scale*, and this *sorry Fellow* WOOD *into the other:* That Mr. WOOD should weigh down *this whole Kingdom*, by which *England* gets above a Million of good Money every Year clear into their *Pockets:* And that is more than the *English* do by *all the World besides*.

But your *great Comfort* is, that, as his Majesty's *Patent* doth not oblige you to take this *Money*, so the *Laws* have not given the *Crown* a Power of forcing the *Subjects* to take what *Money* the *King* pleases:[3] For then by the same Reason we might be bound to take

---

3 A key-argument throughout the *Letters*, i.e. the legal liberty to refuse anything other than gold or silver.

Pebble-stones, or *Cockle-shells*, or *stamped Leather* for *Current Coin*; if ever we should happen to live under an ill *Prince*; who might likewise by the same Power make a *Guinea* pass for Ten Pounds, a *Shilling* for Twenty Shillings, and so on; by which he would in a short Time get all the *Silver* and *Gold* of the *Kingdom* into his own Hands, and leave us nothing but *Brass* or *Leather*, or what he pleased. Neither is any thing reckoned more *Cruel* or *Oppressive* in the *French Government*, than their common Practice of calling in all their Money after they have sunk it very low, and then coining it a-new at a much higher Value; which however is not the Thousandth Part so wicked as this *abominable Project* of Mr. *Wood*. For the *French* give their Subjects *Silver* for *Silver*, and *Gold* for *Gold*; but this *Fellow* will not so much as give us good *Brass* or *Copper* for our *Gold* and *Silver*, nor even a Twelfth Part of their Worth.

Having said this much, I will now go on to tell you the Judgments of some great *Lawyers* in this Matter; whom I fee'd on purpose for your Sakes, and got their *Opinions* under their *Hands*, that I might be sure I went upon good Grounds.

A Famous Law-Book called the Mirrour of Justice, *discoursing of the Charters* (or Laws) *ordained by our* Ancient Kings, *declares the Law to be as follows: It was ordained that no* King *of this Realm should* Change, or Impair *the* Money, *or make any other* Money *than of* Gold *or* Silver *without the Assent of all the Counties, that is,* as my Lord Coke says, * *without the Assent of Parliament.*[4]

This Book is very Ancient, and of great Authority for the Time in which it was wrote, and with that Character is often quoted by that great Lawyer my Lord *Coke*.** By the Laws of *England*, several Metals are divided into *Lawful* or *true Metal* and *unlawful* or *false Metal*; the Former comprehends *Silver* or *Gold*, the Latter all *Baser Metals:* That the Former is only to pass in Payments, appears by an Act of *Parliament**** made the Tweentieth Year of *Edward* the First, called the *Statute concerning the passing of Pence*; which I give you here as I got it translated into *English*; For some of our *Laws* at that time were, as I am told, writ in *Latin: Whoever in Buying or Selling presumeth to refuse an Half-penny or Farthing of Lawful Money, bearing the Stamp which it ought to have, let him be seized on as a Contemner of the King's Majesty, and cast into Prison.*

---

* 2 *Inst.* 576.

** 2 *Inst.* 576. 7.

*** 2 *Inst.* 577.

4 *Mirror of Justices*, a mediaeval compendium of common-law cases. Sir Edward Coke (1552–1634), English judge who opposed abuse of royal prerogative by James I and Charles I.

By this *Statute*, no Person is to be reckoned a *Contemner* of the *King's Majesty*, and for that Crime to be *committed* to *Prison*; but he who refuseth to accept the King's Coin made of *Lawful Metal*: by which as I observed before, *Silver* and *Gold* only are intended.

That this is the true *Construction* of the *Act*, appears not only from the plain Meaning of the Words, but from my Lord *Coke's* * Observation upon it. By this Act (says he) it appears, that no Subject can be forced to take in *Buying* or *Selling* or other *Payments*, any Money made but of lawful Metal; that is, of *Silver* or *Gold*.

The *Law of England* gives the King all Mines of *Gold* and *Silver*, but not the Mines of other *Metals*; the Reason of which *Prerogative* or *Power*, as it is given ** by my Lord *Coke*, is because Money can be made of *Gold* and *Silver*; but not of other Metals.

Pursuant to this Opinion, *Half-pence* and *Farthings* were anciently made of *Silver*, which is evident from the Act of *Parliament* of *Henry* the IVth. Chap. 4. whereby it is enacted as follows: *Item, for the great Scarcity that is at present within the Realm of* England *of Half-pence and Farthings of* Silver; *it is ordained and established, that the Third Part of all the Money of* Silver Plate *which shall be brought to the* Bullion, *shall be made in* Half-pence *and* Farthings. This shews that by the Words *Half-penny* and *Farthing* of Lawful Money in that Statute concerning the *passing of* Pence, is meant a small Coin in *Half-pence* and *Farthings* of *Silver*.

This is further manifest from the Statute of the Ninth Year of *Edward* the IIId. Chap. 3. which enacts, *That no sterling* Half-penny *or* Farthing *be Molten for to make Vessels, or any other thing by the Gold-smiths, nor others, upon Forfeiture of the* Money *so molten (or melted.)*

By another Act in this *King's* Reign, *Black Money* was not to be current in *England*. And by an Act made in the Eleventh Year of his Reign, Chap. 5. *Galley Half-pence* were not to pass: What kind of *Coin* these were I do not know; but I presume they were made of *Base Metal*. And these Acts were no New *Laws*, but further Declarations of the old *Laws* relating to the *Coin*.

Thus the *Law* stands in Relation to *Coin*. Nor is there any Example to the contrary, except one in *Davis's Reports*;[5] who tells us, that in the time of *Tyrone's* Rebellion, *Queen Elizabeth* ordered Money of *mixt Metal* to be coined in the Tower of *London*,

---

* 2 *Inst.* 577.

** 2 *Inst.* 577.

5 Sir John Davies was Attorney-General during the early seventeenth-century plantations in Ireland. Author of *Discovery of the True Causes why Ireland has never been subdued to the English Crown* (1612).

and sent over hither for Payment of the *Army*; obliging all people to receive it; and Commanding, that all *Silver Money* should be taken only as *Bullion*, that is, for as much as it weighed. *Davis* tells us several Particulars in this Matter too long here to trouble you with, and that the *Privy Council* of this *Kingdom* obliged a *Merchant* in *England* to receive this *mixt Money* for Goods transmitted hither.

But this proceeding is rejected by all the best Lawyers, as contrary to Law, the *Privy Council* here having no such legal Power. And besides it is to be considered, that the *Queen* was then under great Difficulties by a Rebellion in this *Kingdom* assisted from *Spain*. And, whatever is done in great Exigences and dangerous Times, should never be an Example to proceed by in Seasons of *Peace* and *Quietness*.

I will now, my dear Friends, to save you the Trouble, set before you in short, what the *Law* obliges you to do; and what it does not oblige you to.

First, you are obliged to take all Money in Payments which is coined by the *King*, and is of the *English* Standard or Weight; provided it be of *Gold* or *Silver*.

Secondly, you are not obliged to take any Money which is not of *Gold* or *Silver*; not only the *Half-pence* or *Farthings* of *England*, but of any other Country. And it is meerly for Convenience, or Ease, that you are content to take them; because the Custom of coining *Silver Half-pence* and *Farthings* hath long been left off; I suppose, on Account of their being subject to be lost.

Thirdly, Much less are we obliged to take those *Vile Half-pence* of that same *Wood*, by which you must lose almost Eleven-Pence in every Shilling.

Therefore, my Friends, stand to it One and All: Refuse this *Filthy Trash*. It is no Treason to rebel against Mr. *Wood*. His *Majesty* in his Patent obliges no body to take these *Half-pence*: Our *Gracious Prince* hath no such ill Advisers about him; or if he had, yet you see the Laws have not left it in the *King's* Power, to force us to take any Coin but what is Lawful, of right Standard, *Gold* and *Silver*. Therefore you have nothing to fear.

And let me in the next Place apply my self particularly to you who are the poorer Sort of *Tradesmen*: Perhaps you may think you will not be so great Losers as the Rich, if these *Half-pence* should pass; because you seldom see any *Silver*, and your Customers come to your Shops or Stalls with nothing but *Brass*; which you likewise find hard to be got. But you may take my Word, whenever this Money gains Footing among you, you will be utterly undone. If you carry these *Half-pence* to a Shop for *Tobacco* or *Brandy*, or any other Thing you want; the Shop-keeper will advance his Goods accordingly, or else he must break and leave the *Key under the Door.* Do you think I will sell you a Yard of Ten-penny Stuff for Twenty of Mr *Wood's Half-pence?* No, not under Two Hundred at least; neither will I be at the Trouble of counting, but weigh them in a Lump. I will tell you one Thing further; that if Mr. *Wood's* Project should take, it will ruin even our Beggars: For when I give a Beggar a Half-penny, it will quench his Thirst, or go a good Way to fill his Belly; but the Twelfth Part of a Half-penny will do him no more Service than if I should give him three Pins out of my Sleeve.

In short; these *Half-pence* are like the *accursed Thing,* which, as the *Scripture* tells us, the *Children of Israel* were forbidden to touch.[6] They will run about like the *Plague* and destroy every one who lays his Hands upon them. I have heard *Scholars* talk of a Man who told the King that he had invented a Way to torment People by putting them into a *Bull* of Brass with Fire under it: But the *Prince* put the *Projector* first into his own *Brazen Bull* to make the Experiment. This very much resembles the Project of Mr. *Wood;* and the like of this may possibly be Mr. *Wood's* Fate; that the *Brass* he contrived to torment this *Kingdom* with, may prove his own Torment, and his Destruction at last.

N.B. The Author of this Paper is informed by Persons who have made it their Business to be exact in their Observations on the true Value of these *Half-pence;* that any Person may expect to get a Quart of Two-penny Ale for Thirty Six of them.

I desire that all Families may keep this Paper carefully by them to refresh their Memories whenever they shall have farther Notice of Mr. Wood's Half-pence, or any other the like Imposture.

---

6 Joshua 6:18. The subsequent verse has an even more explicit application: 'But all the silver, and gold, and vessels of brass and iron, are consecrated unto the LORD: they shall come into the treasury of the LORD.'

LETTER IV

To the whole People
of *IRELAND.*

This pamphlet, the fourth of the *Drapier's Letters*, appeared on 22 October 1724, and proved the most controversial of the campaign. Because of its loud declarations on behalf of Irish legislative independence, it was immediately prosecuted for sedition. The printer, (as with the 1720 *Proposal*), was arrested, and a reward of £300 offered for identifying the author. The reward was never claimed. The rhetorical ambition of the pamphlet's title is deceptive, since Swift is largely addressing the Protestant and propertied interest.

LETTER IV

To the whole People
of *IRELAND*.

N.B. *This was the Letter against which the Lord Lieutenant* (Carteret) *and Council, issued a Proclamation, offering three Hundred Pounds to discover the Author; and for which,* Harding *the Printer was tried before one* Whitshed, *then Chief Justice: But the noble Jury would not find the Bill; nor would any Person discover the Author.*

My dear Countrymen,

HAVING already written three *Letters,* upon so disagreeable a Subject as Mr. *Wood* and his *Half-pence;* I conceived my task was at an End: But, I find that Cordials must be frequently applied to weak Constitutions *Political* as well as *Natural.* A People long used to Hardships, lose by Degrees the very Notions of *Liberty;* they look upon themselves as Creatures at Mercy; and that all Impositions laid on them by a stronger Hand, are, in the Phrase of the *Report, legal* and *obligatory.* Hence proceed that *Poverty* and *Lowness of Spirit,* to which a *Kingdom* may be subject, as well as a *particular Person.* And when *Esau* came fainting from the Field, at the Point to dye, it is no Wonder that he sold his *Birth-Right for a Mess of Pottage.*

I thought I had sufficiently shewn to all who could want Instruction, by what Methods they might safely proceed, whenever this *Coin* should be offered to them: And, I believe, there hath not been, for many Ages, an Example of any Kingdom so firmly united in a Point of great Importance, as this of ours is at present, against that detestable Fraud. But, however, it so happens, that some weak People begin to be alarmed a-new, by Rumours industriously spread. *Wood* prescribes to the News-Mongers in *London,* what they are to write. In one of their Papers published here by some obscure Printer, (and certainly with a bad Design) we are told, that the *Papists in* Ireland *have entered into an Association against his Coin;* although it be notoriously known, that they never once offered to stir in the Matter: So that the two Houses of Parliament, the Privy-Council, the great Numbers of Corporations, the Lord-Mayor and Aldermen of *Dublin*, the Grand-Juries, and principal Gentlemen of several Counties, are stigmatized in a Lump, under the Name of *Papists*.

This Impostor and his Crew, do likewise give out, that, by refusing to receive his Dross for Sterling, we *dispute the King's Prerogative; are grown ripe for Rebellion, and ready to shake off the Dependency of* Ireland *upon the Crown of* England. To countenance which Reports, he hath published a Paragraph in another News-Paper, to let us know, that *the Lord Lieutenant is ordered to come over immediately to settle his Half-pence.*

I intreat you, my dear Countrymen, not to be under the least Concern upon these and the like Rumours; which are no more than the last Howls of a Dog dissected alive, as I hope he hath sufficiently been. These Calumnies are the only Reserve that is left him. For surely, our continued and (almost) unexampled Loyalty, will never be called in Question, for not suffering our selves to be robbed of all that we have, by one obscure *Ironmonger*.

As to disputing the King's *Prerogative*, give me Leave to explain to those who are ignorant, what the Meaning of that Word *Prerogative* is.

The Kings of these Realms enjoy several Powers, wherein the Laws have not interposed: So, they can make War and Peace without the Consent of Parliament; and this is a very great *Prerogative*. But if the Parliament doth not approve of the War, the King must bear the Charge of it out of his own Purse; and this is as great a Check on the Crown. So the King hath a *Prerogative* to coin Money, without Consent of Parliament: But he cannot compel the Subject to take that Money, except it be Sterling, Gold or Silver; because, herein he is limited by Law. Some Princes have, indeed, extended their *Prerogative* further than the Law allowed them: Wherein, however, the Lawyers of succeeding Ages, as fond as they are of *Precedents*, have never dared to justify them. But, to say the Truth, it is only of late Times that *Prerogative* hath been fixed and ascertained. For, whoever reads the Histories of *England*, will find that some former Kings, and those none of the worst, have, upon several Occasions, ventured to controul the Laws, with very little Ceremony or Scruple, even later than the Days of Queen *Elizabeth*. In her Reign, that pernicious Counsel of sending *base Money* hither, very narrowly failed of losing the Kingdom; being complained of by the Lord Deputy, the Council, and the whole Body of the *English* here: So that soon after her Death, it was recalled by her Successor, and lawful Money paid in Exchange.

Having thus given you some Notion of what is meant by the King's *Prerogative*, as far as a *Tradesman* can be thought capable of explaining it, I will only add the Opinion of the great Lord *Bacon*; that, *as God governs the World by the settled Laws of Nature, which he hath made, and never transcends those Laws, but upon high important Occasions: So, among earthly Princes, those are the Wisest and the Best, who govern by the known Laws of the Country, and seldomest make Use of their* Prerogative.[1]

Now, here you may see that the vile Accusation of *Wood* and his Accomplices, charging us with *disputing the King's Prerogative* by refusing his Brass, can have no Place; because compelling the Subject to take any Coin, which is not Sterling, is no Part of the King's *Prerogative*; and I am very confident, if it were so, we should be the last of his People to dispute it; as well from that inviolable Loyalty we have always paid to his Majesty, as from the Treatment we might in such a Case justly expect from some, who seem to think, we have neither *common Sense*, nor *common Senses*. But, God be thanked, the best of them are only our *Fellow-Subjects*, and not our *Masters*. One great Merit I am sure we have, which those of *English* Birth can have no Pretence to; that our Ancestors reduced this Kingdom to the Obedience of ENGLAND; for which we have been rewarded with a worse Climate, the Privilege of being governed by Laws to which we do not consent; a ruined Trade, a House of *Peers* without *Jurisdiction*; almost an Incapacity for all Employments, and the Dread of *Wood's* Half-pence.

But we are so far from disputing the King's *Prerogative* in coining, that we own he hath Power to give a Patent to any Man, for setting his Royal Image and Superscription upon whatever Materials he pleases; and Liberty to the Patentee to offer them in any Country from *England* to *Japan*; only attended with one small Limitation, that *no body alive is obliged to take them*.

Upon these Considerations, I was ever against all Recourse to *England* for a Remedy against the present impending Evil; especially, when I observed, that the Addresses of both Houses, after long Expectance, produced nothing but a REPORT altogether in Favour of *Wood*; upon which, I made some Observations in a former Letter;[2] and might at least have made as many more: For, it is a Paper of as singular a Nature as I ever beheld.

1 Not, as far as I can discover, a direct quotation from Bacon, but a polemical version of his general belief in the benign authority of the monarch with regard to legal custom.
2 The English Ministry, under increasing pressure from Ireland, had produced an official *Report* on Wood's enterprise. Published on 6 August 1724, it completely vindicated the conduct of the patent. A scornful Swift promptly wrote *Some Observations upon a Report*, the third of the *Letters*, which appeared on the 25 August. It was subtitled, 'To the Nobility and Gentry of the Kingdom of Ireland.'

But I mistake; for before this *Report* was made, his Majesty's *most gracious Answer* to the House of Lords was sent over, and printed; wherein there are these Words, *granting the Patent for coining Half-pence and Farthings*, AGREEABLE TO THE PRACTICE OF HIS ROYAL PREDECESSORS, &c. That King *Charles* II, and King *James* II, (AND THEY ONLY) did grant Patents for this Purpose, is indisputable, and I have shewn it at large. Their Patents were passed under the great Seal of *Ireland*, by References to *Ireland*; the Copper to be coined in *Ireland*, the Patentee was bound, on Demand, to receive his Coin back in *Ireland*, and pay Silver and Gold in Return. *Wood's* Patent was made under the great Seal of *England*, the Brass coined in *England*, not the least Reference made to *Ireland*; the Sum immense, and the Patentee under no Obligation to receive it again, and give good Money for it: This I only mention, because, in my private Thoughts, I have sometimes made a Query, whether the *Penner* of those Words in his Majesty's *most gracious Answer*, AGREEABLE TO THE PRACTICE OF HIS ROYAL PREDECESSORS, had maturely considered the several Circumstances; which, in my poor Opinion, seem to make a Difference.

Let me now say something concerning the other great Cause of some People's Fear; as *Wood* has taught the *London* News-Writer to express it: That *his Excellency the Lord Lieutenant is coming over to settle* Wood's *Half-pence.*[3]

We know very well, that the Lords Lieutenants, for several Years past, have not thought this Kingdom *worthy the Honour of their Residence*, longer than was absolutely necessary for the King's Business; which consequently *wanted no Speed in the Dispatch*. And therefore, it naturally fell into most Mens Thoughts, that a new Governor coming at an *unusual* Time, must portend some *unusual* Business to be done; especially, if the common Report be true; that the Parliament prorogued to I know not when, is, by a new Summons (revoking that Prorogation) to assemble soon after his Arrival: For which extraordinary Proceeding, the Lawyers on t'other Side the Water, have, by great good Fortune, found two *Precedents*.

All this being granted, it can never enter into my Head, that so *little a Creature as Wood* could find Credit enough with the King and his Ministers, to have the Lord Lieutenant of *Ireland* sent hither in a Hurry, upon his Errand.

For, let us take the whole Matter nakedly, as it lies before us,

---

3 Lord Cartaret, who had replaced the ineffectual Duke of Grafton, was a friend of Swift, the two having met at the Court of Queen Anne when Swift was writing for the Tory party. Their familiarity lent a delicate personal dimension to the political controversy.

without the Refinements of some People, with which we have nothing to do. Here is a Patent granted under the great Seal of *England*, upon false Suggestions, to one *William Wood*, for coining Copper Half-pence for *Ireland:* The Parliament here, upon Apprehensions of the worst Consequences from the said Patent, address the King to have it recalled: This is refused, and a Committee of the Privy-Council *report* to his Majesty, that *Wood* has performed the Conditions of his Patent. He then is left to do the best he can with his Half-pence; no Man being obliged to receive them; the People here, being likewise left to themselves, unite as one Man; resolving they will have nothing to do with his Ware. By this plain Account of the Fact, it is manifest, that the King and his Ministry are wholly out of the Case; and the Matter is left to be disputed between him and us. Will any Man therefore attempt to persuade me, that a Lord Lieutenant is to be dispatched over in great Haste, before the ordinary Time, and a Parliament summoned, by anticipating a Prorogation; merely to put an Hundred Thousand Pounds into the Pocket of a *Sharper*, by the Ruin of a most loyal Kingdom?

But supposing all this to be true. By what Arguments could a Lord Lieutenant prevail on the same Parliament, which addressed with so much Zeal and Earnestness against this Evil; to pass it into a Law? I am sure their Opinion of *Wood* and his Project are not mended since their last Prorogation: And supposing those *Methods* should be used, which, *Detractors* tell us, have been sometimes put in Practice for *gaining Votes*; it is well known, that in this Kingdom there are few Employments to be given; and if there were more; it is *as well known* to whose Share they must fall.

But, because great Numbers of you are altogether ignorant in the Affairs of your Country, I will tell you some Reasons, why there are so few Employments to be disposed of in this Kingdom. All considerable Offices for Life here, are possessed by those, to whom the Reversions were granted; and these have been generally Followers of the Chief Governors, or Persons who had Interest in the Court of *England*. So the Lord *Berkely* of *Stratton*, holds that great Office of *Master of the Rolls*; the Lord *Palmerstown* is *First Remembrancer*, worth near 2000 *l. per Ann.* One *Dodington*, Secretary to the Earl of *Pembroke*, begged the Reversion of *Clerk of the Pells*, worth 2500 *l.* a Year, which he now enjoys by the Death of the Lord *Newtown*. Mr. *Southwell* is Secretary of State, and the Earl of *Burlington* Lord High Treasurer of *Ireland* by Inheritance. These are only a few among many others, which I have been told of, but cannot remember. Nay the Reversion of several Employments during Pleasure are granted the same Way. This among many others, is a

Circumstance whereby the Kingdom of *Ireland* is distinguished from all other Nations upon Earth; and makes it so difficult an Affair to get into a Civil Employ, that Mr. *Addison* was forced to purchase an old obscure Place, called *Keeper of the Records in* Bermingham's *Tower*, of Ten Pounds a Year, and to get a Salary of 400 *l.* annexed to it, though all the Records there are not worth Half a Crown, either for Curiosity or Use. And we lately saw a * *Favourite Secretary*, descend to be *Master of the Revels*, which by his *Credit and Extortion* he hath made *Pretty Considerable*. I say nothing of the Under-Treasurership worth about 9000 *l.* a Year; nor the Commissioners of the Revenue, Four of whom generally live in *England:* For I think none of these are granted in Reversion. But the Jest is, that I have known upon Occasion, some of these absent Officers as *Keen* against the Interest of *Ireland*, as if they had never been indebted to Her for a *Single Groat*.

I confess, I have been sometimes tempted to wish that this Project of *Wood* might succeed; because I reflected with some Pleasure, what a *Jolly Crew* it would bring over among us of *Lords* and *Squires*, and *Pensioners* of *Both Sexes*, and Officers *Civil* and *Military*; where we should live together as merry and sociable as Beggars; only with this one Abatement, that we should neither have *Meat* to feed, nor *Manufactures* to Cloath us; unless we could be content to *Prance* about in *Coats of Mail*; or eat Brass as Ostritches do Iron.

I return from this Digression, to that which gave me the Occasion of making it: And I believe you are now convinced, that if the Parliament of *Ireland* were as *Temptable* as any *other* Assembly, *within a Mile* of Christendom (which God forbids) yet the *Managers* must of Necessity fail for want of *Tools* to work with. But I will yet go one Step further, by Supposing that a Hundred new Employments, were erected on Purpose to gratify *Compliers*: Yet still an insuperable Difficulty would remain. For it happens, I know not how, that *Money* is neither *Whig* nor *Tory*, neither of *Town* nor *Country Party*; and it is not improbable, that a Gentleman would rather chuse to live upon his *own Estate*, which brings him *Gold* and *Silver*, than with the Addition of an *Employment*; when his *Rents* and *Sallary* must both be paid in *Wood's* Brass, at above Eighty *per Cent.* Discount.

For these, and many other Reasons , I am confident you need not be under the least Apprehensions, from the sudden Expectation of the *Lord Lieutenant*, while we continue in our present hearty Disposition; to alter which, there is no suitable Temptation can

---

* Mr. Hopkins, *Secretary to the Duke of* Grafton.

possibly be offered: And if, as I have often asserted from the best Authority, the *Law* hath not left a *Power* in the *Crown* to force any Money, except Sterling, upon the Subject; much less can the Crown *devolve* such a *Power* upon *another*.

This I speak with the utmost Respect to the *Person* and *Dignity* of his Excellency the Lord *Carteret*; whose Character was lately given me, by a Gentleman that hath known him from his first Appearance in the World: That Gentleman describes him as a young Man of great Accomplishments, excellent Learning, Regular in his Life, and of much Spirit and Vivacity. He hath since, as I have heard, been employed abroad; was principal Secretary of State; and is now about the 37th Year of his Age appointed Lord Lieutenant of *Ireland*. From such a Governour this Kingdom may reasonably hope for as much Prosperity, *as under so many Discouragements* it can be capable of receiving.

It is true indeed, that within the Memory of Man, there have been Governors of so much Dexterity, as to carry Points of terrible Consequence to this Kingdom, by their Power with *those who are in Office*; and by their Arts in managing or deluding others with *Oaths, Affability*, and even with *Dinners*. If *Wood's* Brass had, in those Times, been upon the *Anvil*, it is obvious enough to conceive what Methods would have been taken. *Depending* Persons would have been told in plain Terms, that it was a *Service expected from them, under the Pain of the publick Business being put into more complying Hands*. Others would be allured by *Promises*. To the *Country Gentlemen*, besides *good Words, Burgundy* and *Closeting*; it might, perhaps, have been hinted, how *kindly it would be taken to comply with a Royal Patent, although it were not compulsary*. That if any Inconveniences ensued, it might be made up with other *Graces or Favours hereafter: That Gentlemen ought to consider, whether it were prudent or safe to disgust* England: They would be desired to *think of some good Bills for encouraging of Trade, and setting the Poor to work: Some further Acts against Popery, and for uniting Protestants*. There would be solemn Engagements, that we should *never be troubled with above Forty Thousand Pounds in his Coin, and all of the best and weightiest Sort; for which we should only give our Manufactures in Exchange, and keep our Gold and Silver at home*. Perhaps, *a seasonable Report of some Invasion would have been spread in the most proper Juncture*; which is a great Smoother of Rubs in publick Proceedings: And we should have been told, that *this was no Time to create Differences, when the Kingdom was in Danger*.

THESE, I say, and the like Methods, would, in corrupt Times, have been taken to let in this Deluge of Brass among us: And, I am confident, would even then have not succeeded; much less under the Administration of so excellent a Person as the Lord *Carteret*; and in a Country, where the People of all Ranks, Parties, and Denominations, are convinced to a Man, that the utter undoing of themselves and their Posterity for ever, will be dated from the Admission of that execrable Coin: That if it once enters, it can be no more confined to a small or moderate Quantity, than the *Plague* can be confined to a few Families; and that no *Equivalent* can be given by any earthly Power, any more than a dead Carcass can be recovered to Life by a Cordial.

There is one comfortable Circumstance in this universal Opposition to Mr. *Wood*, that the People sent over hither from *England*, to *fill up our Vacancies, Ecclesiastical, Civil and Military*, are all on our Side: *Money*, the great *Divider* of the World, hath, by a strange Revolution, been the great *Uniter* of a most *divided* People. Who would leave a Hundred Pounds a Year in *England*, *(a Country of Freedom)* to be paid a Thousand in *Ireland* out of *Wood's* Exchequer? The *Gentleman They* have lately made *Primate*,[4] would never quit his Seat in an *English* House of Lords, and his Preferments at *Oxford* and *Bristol*, worth Twelve Hundred Pounds a Year, for four Times the Denomination here, but not half the Value: Therefore, I expect to hear he will be as good an *Irishman*, at least, upon *this one Article*, as any of his Brethren; or even of *Us*, who have had the *Misfortune* to be born in this Island. For those who, in the common Phrase, do not *come hither to learn the Language*, would never change a better Country for a worse, to receive *Brass* instead of *Gold*.

Another Slander spread by *Wood* and his Emissaries is, that, by opposing him, we discover an Inclination to *shake off our Dependance upon the Crown of* England. Pray observe, how important a Person is this same *William Wood*; and how the publick Weal of two Kingdoms, is involved in his private Interest. First, all those who refuse to take his Coin *are Papists*; for he tells us, that *none but Papists are associated against him*. Secondly, they *dispute the King's Prerogative*. Thirdly, they *are ripe for Rebellion*. And Fourthly, they are going to *shake off their Dependance upon the Crown of* England; that is to say, *they are going to chuse another King:* For there can be no other Meaning in this Expression, however some may pretend to strain it.

And this gives me an Opportunity of explaining, to those who

4 Hugh Boulter, Bishop of Bristol, succeeded Thomas Lindsay as Primate of Ireland during the summer of 1724. Swift regarded him as yet another pro-London appointee.

are ignorant, another Point, which hath often *swelled in my Breast*. Those who come over hither to us from *England*, and some *weak* People among ourselves, whenever, in Discourse, we make mention of *Liberty* and *Property*, shake their Heads, and tell us, that *Ireland* is a *depending Kingdom*; as if they would seem, by this Phrase, to intend, that the People of *Ireland* is in some State of Slavery or Dependance, different from those of *England*: whereas, a *depending Kingdom* is a *modern Term of Art*; unknown, as I have heard, to all antient *Civilians*, and *Writers upon Government*;[5] and *Ireland* is, on the contrary called in some Statutes an *Imperial Crown*, as held only from God; which is as high a Style, as any Kingdom is capable of receiving. Therefore by this Expression, a *depending Kingdom*, there is no more understood, than that by a Statute made here, in the 33d Year of *Henry VIII, The King and his Successors, are to be Kings Imperial of this Realm, as united and knit to the Imperial Crown of* England. I have looked over all the *English* and *Irish* Statutes, without finding any Law that makes *Ireland depend* upon *England*; any more than *England* doth upon *Ireland. We have, indeed, obliged ourselves to have the same King with them*; and consequently they are obliged to have the *same King with us*. For the Law was made by *our own Parliament*; and our Ancestors then were not such *Fools (whatever they were in the preceding Reign)* to bring themselves under I know not what *Dependance*, which is now talked of, without any Ground of *Law, Reason*, or *common Sense*.

Let whoever think otherwise, I *M. B. Drapier*,[6] desire to be excepted. For I declare, next under God, I *depend* only on the King my Sovereign, and on the Laws of my own Country. And I am so far from *depending* upon the People of *England*, that, if they should ever *rebel* against my Sovereign, (which GOD forbid) I would be ready at the first Command from his Majesty, to take Arms against them; as some of *my* Countrymen did against *theirs* at *Preston*. And, if such a Rebellion should prove so successful as to fix the *Pretender* on the Throne of *England*; I would venture to transgress that *Statute* so far, as to lose every Drop of my Blood, to hinder him from being *King of Ireland*.

It is true, indeed, that within the Memory of Man, the Parliaments of *England* have *sometimes* assumed the Power of binding this Kingdom, by Laws enacted there; wherein they were, at first, openly opposed (as far as *Truth, Reason*, and *Justice* are capable of

---

5 Here Swift deliberately ignores the Declaratory Act of 1720 which expressly defined Ireland as a 'dependent' kingdom, a status he never accepted.

6 The Drapier's initials, M. B., probably allude to Marcus Brutus, one of Swift's favourite models of civic and political virtue.

opposing) by the famous Mr. *Molineaux* an *English* Gentleman born here;[7] as well as by several of the greatest Patriots, and *best Whigs* in *England*; but the *Love and Torrent* of Power prevailed. Indeed, the Arguments on both Sides were invincible. For in *Reason*, all *Government* without the Consent of the *Governed*, is the *very Definition of Slavery*: But in *Fact, Eleven Men well armed, will certainly subdue one single Man in his Shirt*. But I have done. For those who have used *Power* to cramp *Liberty*, have gone so far as to resent even the *Liberty* of *Complaining*; although a Man upon the Rack, was never known to be refused the Liberty of *roaring* as loud as he thought fit.

And, as we are apt to *sink* too *much* under *unreasonable* Fears, so we are too soon inclined to be *raised* by groundless Hopes, (according to the Nature of all *consumptive* Bodies like ours.) Thus, it hath been given about for several Days past, that *Somebody* in *England*, empowered a second *Somebody* to write to a third *Somebody* here, to assure us, that we *should no more be troubled with those Half-pence*. And this is reported to have been done by the * *same Person*, who was said to have sworn some Months ago, that he would *ram them down our Throats*. (though I doubt they would *stick in our Stomachs*) But which ever of these Reports is true or false, it is no Concern of ours. For, *in this Point*, we have nothing to do with *English Ministers*: And I should be sorry to leave it in their Power to *redress* this Grievance, or to *enforce* it: For the *Report of the Committee* hath given me a *Surfeit*. The Remedy is wholly in your own Hands; and therefore I have digressed a little, in order to refresh and continue that *Spirit* so seasonably raised amongst you; and to let you see, that by the Laws of GOD, of NATURE, of NATIONS, and of your own Country, you ARE and OUGHT to be as FREE a People as your Brethren in *England*.

If the Pamphlets published at *London* by *Wood* and his *Journeymen*, in Defence of his Cause, were Re-printed here, and that our Countrymen could be persuaded to read them, they would convince you of his wicked Design, more than all I shall ever be able to say. In short, I make him a perfect *Saint*, in Comparison of what he appears to be, from the Writings of those whom he *Hires* to justify his *Project*. But he is so far *Master of the Field (let others guess the*

* *Mr. Walpole, now Sir Robert.*

7 William Molyneux (1656–98). Philosopher, friend and correspondent of Locke, and M.P. for Trinity College Dublin. His pamphlet, *The Case of Ireland's Being Bound by Acts of Parliament in England, Stated* (1698), was the original declaration of Ireland's claim to legislative independence. The pamphlet had been declared illegal and seditious.

Reason) that no *London* Printer dare publish any Paper written in Favour of *Ireland:* And here no Body hath yet been so *bold* as to publish any Thing in *Favour* of *him.*

There was a few Days ago a Pamphlet sent me of near 50 Pages, written in Favour of Mr. *Wood* and his Coinage; printed in *London:* It is not worth answering, because probably it will never be published here: But it gave me an Occasion, to reflect upon an Unhappiness we lie under, that the People of *England* are utterly ignorant of our Case: Which, however, is no Wonder; since it is a Point they do not in the least concern themselves about; farther than, perhaps, as a Subject of Discourse in a Coffee-House, when they have nothing else to talk of. For I have Reason to believe, that no Minister ever gave himself the Trouble of reading any Papers written in our Defence; because I suppose *their Opinions are already determined*, and are formed wholly upon the Reports of *Wood* and his Accomplices; else it would be impossible, that any Man could have the Impudence, to write such a Pamphlet, as I have mentioned.

Our *Neighbours, whose Understandings are just upon a Level with Ours* (which perhaps are none of the *Brightest*) have a strong Contempt for most Nations, but especially for *Ireland:* They look upon us as a Sort of *Savage Irish,* whom our Ancestors conquered several Hundred Years ago: And if I should describe the *Britons* to you, as they were in *Caesar's* Time, when they *painted their Bodies, or cloathed themselves with the Skins of Beasts,* I should act full as reasonably as they do. However, they are so far to be excused, in relation to the present Subject, that, hearing only *one Side of the Cause,* and having neither Opportunity nor Curiosity to examine the *other,* they *believe a Lye,* merely for their Ease; and conclude, because Mr. *Wood* pretends to have *Power,* he hath also *Reason* on his Side.

Therefore, to let you see how this Case is represented in *England* by *Wood* and his Adherents, I have thought it proper to extract out of that Pamphlet, a few of those notorious Falsehoods, in Point of *Fact* and *Reasoning,* contained therein; the Knowledge whereof, will confirm my Countrymen in their *Own* Right Sentiments, when they will see by comparing both, how much their *Enemies are in the Wrong.*

First, The Writer positively asserts, *That* Wood's *Half-pence were current among us for several Months, with the universal Approbation of all People, without one single Gain sayer; and we all to a Man thought our selves Happy in having them.*

Secondly, He affirms, *That we were drawn into a Dislike of them, only by some Cunning Evil-designing Men among us, who opposed this Patent of* Wood, *to get another for themselves.*

Thirdly, That *those who most declared at first against* WOOD'S *Patent, were the very Men who intend to get another for their own Advantage.*

Fourthly, That *our Parliament and Privy-Council, the Lord Mayor and Aldermen of* Dublin, *the Grand-Juries and Merchants, and in short the whole Kingdom; nay, the very Dogs* (as he expresseth it) *were fond of those Half-pence, till they were inflamed by those few designing Persons aforesaid.*

Fifthly, He says directly, That *all those who opposed the Half-pence, were Papists, and Enemies to King* George.

Thus far I am confident, the most ignorant among you can safely swear from your own Knowledge, that the Author is a most notorious Lyar in every Article; the direct contrary being so manifest to the whole Kingdom, that if Occasion required, we might get it confirmed *under Five hundred thousand Hands.*

Sixthly, He would persuade us, That *if we sell Five Shillings worth of our Goods or Manufactures for Two Shillings and Four-pence worth of Copper, although the Copper were melted down, and that we could get Five Shillings in Gold and Silver for the said Goods; yet to take the said Two Shillings and Four-pence in Copper, would be greatly for our Advantage.*

And Lastly, He makes us a very fair Offer, as empowered by *Wood,* That *if we will take off Two hundred thousand Pounds in his Half-pence for our Goods, and likewise pay him Three* per Cent. *Interest for Thirty Years, for an hundred and Twenty thousand Pounds (at which he computes the Coinage above the intrinsick Value of the Copper) for the Loan of his Coin, he will after that Time give us good Money for what Half-pence will be then left.*

Let me place this Offer in as clear a Light as I can, to shew the unsupportable Villainy and Impudence of that incorrigible Wretch. First (says he) *I will send Two hundred thousand Pounds of my Coin into your Country: The Copper I compute to be in real Value Eighty thousand Pounds, and I charge you with an hundred and twenty thousand Pounds for the Coinage; so that you see, I lend you an Hundred and twenty thousand Pounds for Thirty Years; for which you shall pay me Three* per Cent. *That is to say, Three thousand Six hundred Pounds,* per Ann. *which in Thirty Years will amount to an Hundred and eight thousand Pounds. And when these Thirty Years are expired, return me my Copper, and I will give you Good Money for it.*

This is the Proposal made to us by *Wood* in that Pamphlet, written by one of his *Commissioners:* And the Author is supposed to be the same Infamous *Coleby* one of his *Under-Swearers* at the *Committee of Council*, who was tryed for *Robbing the Treasury here*, where he was an Under-Clerk.

By this Proposal he will first receive Two hundred thousand Pounds, in Goods or Sterling, for as much Copper as he values at Eighty thousand Pounds; but in Reality not worth Thirty thousand Pounds. Secondly, He will receive for Interest an Hundred and Eight thousand Pounds: And when our Children come Thirty Years hence, to return his Half-pence upon his Executors (for before that Time he will be probably gone *to his own Place*) those Executors will very reasonably reject them as Raps and Counterfeits; which they will be, and Millions of them of his own Coinage.

Methinks, I am fond of such a *Dealer* as this, who mends every Day upon our Hands, like a *Dutch* Reckoning; where, if you dispute the Unreasonableness and Exorbitance of the Bill, the Landlord shall bring it up every Time with new Additions.

Although these and the like Pamphlets, published by *Wood* in *London*, be altogether unknown here, where no body could read them, without as much *Indignation* as *Contempt* would allow; yet I thought it proper to give you a Specimen how the *Man* employs his Time; where he Rides alone without any Creature to contradict him; while OUR FEW FRIENDS there wonder at our Silence: And the *English* in general, if they think of this Matter at all, impute our Refusal to *Wilfulness* or *Disaffection*, just as *Wood* and his *Hirelings* are pleased to represent.

But although our Arguments are not suffered to be printed in *England*, yet the Consequence will be of little Moment. Let *Wood* endeavour to *persuade* the People *There*, that we ought to *Receive* his Coin; and let Me *Convince* our People *Here*, that they ought to *Reject* it under Pain of our utter Undoing. And then let him do his *Best* and his *Worst*.

Before I conclude, I must beg Leave, in all Humility to tell Mr. *Wood*, that he is guilty of great *Indiscretion*, by causing so Honourable a Name as that of Mr. *Walpole* to be mentioned so often, and in such a Manner, upon his Occasion. A short Paper, printed at *Bristol*, and re-printed here, reports Mr. *Wood* to say, that he *wonders at the Impudence and Insolence of the* Irish, *in refusing his Coin, and what he will do when Mr.* Walpole *comes to Town.* Where, by the Way, he is mistaken; for it is the *True English People* of *Ireland*, who refuse it; although we take it for granted, that the *Irish* will do so too, whenever they are asked. In another printed Paper of his contriving, it is roundly expressed, that Mr. *Walpole will cram his Brass down our Throats.* Sometimes it is given out, that we must *either take these Half-pence or eat our Brogues*, And, in another News-Letter but of Yesterday, we read, that the same great Man *hath sworn to make us swallow his Coin in Fire-Balls*.

This brings to my Mind the known Story of a *Scotch Man*, who receiving Sentence of Death, with all the Circumstances of *Hanging, Beheading, Quartering, Embowelling*, and the like; cried out, *What need all this* COOKERY? And I think we have Reason to ask the same Question: For if we believe *Wood*, here is a *Dinner* getting ready for us, and you see the *Bill of Fare*; and I am sorry the *Drink* was forgot, which might easily be supplied with *Melted Lead* and *Flaming Pitch*.

What vile Words are these to put into the Mouth of a great Counsellor, in high Trust with his Majesty, and looked upon as a prime Minister? If Mr. *Wood* hath no better a Manner of representing his Patrons; when I come to be a *Great Man*, he shall never be suffered to attend at my *Levee*. This is not the Style of a Great Minister; it savours too much of the *Kettle* and the *Furnace*; and came entirely out of *Wood's Forge*.

As for the Threat of making us *eat our Brogues*, we need not be in Pain; for if his Coin should pass, that *Unpolite Covering for the Feet*, would no longer *be a National Reproach*; because, then we should have neither *Shoe* nor *Brogue* left in the Kingdom. But here the Falshood of Mr. *Wood* is fairly detected; for I am confident Mr. *Walpole* never heard of a *Brogue* in his whole Life.

As to *Swallowing these Half-pence in Fire-balls*, it is a Story equally improbable. For, to execute this *Operation*, the whole Stock of Mr. *Wood's* Coin and Metal must be melted down, and molded into hollow *Balls* with *Wild-fire*, no bigger than a *reasonable* Throat can be able to swallow.[8] Now, the Metal he hath prepared, and already coined, will amount to at least Fifty Millions of Half-pence to be *Swallowed* by a Million and a Half of People; so that allowing Two Half-pence to each *Ball*, there will be about Seventeen *Balls* of *Wild-fire* a-piece, to be swallowed by every Person in the Kingdom: And to administer this Dose, there cannot be conveniently fewer than Fifty thousand *Operators*, allowing one *Operator* to every Thirty; which, considering the *Squeamishness* of some Stomachs, and the *Peevishness* of *Young Children*, is but reasonable. Now, under Correction of better Judgments, I think the Trouble and Charge of such an Experiment, would exceed the Profit; and therefore I take this *Report* to be *spurious*; or, at least, only a new *Scheme* of Mr. *Wood* himself; which, to make it pass the better in *Ireland*, he would Father upon a *Minister of State*.

8 Here begin the kind of mock-calculations later developed by Swift in *A Modest Proposal*.

But I will now demonstrate, beyond all Contradiction, that Mr. *Walpole* is against this Project of Mr. *Wood*; and is an entire Friend to *Ireland*; only by this one invincible Argument. That he has the Universal Opinion of being a wise Man, an able Minister, and in all his Proceedings, pursuing the *True Interest* of the *King his Master*: And that, as his *Integrity* is above all *Corruption*, so is his *Fortune* above all *Temptation*. I reckon therefore, we are perfectly safe from that *Corner*; and shall never be under the Necessity of Contending with so *Formidable a Power*; but be left to possess our *Brogues* and *Potatoes* in *Peace*, as * *Remote from Thunder as we are from Jupiter*.

I am, My dear Countrymen, your Loving Fellow-
Subject, Fellow-Sufferer, and Humble Servant,

Oct. 13, 1724.   M. B.

* *Procul à Jove, procul à fulmine.*

A
LETTER

To the Right Honourable the
Lord Viscount *Molesworth*.

They compassed me about also with Words of Deceit, and fought against me without a Cause.

For my Love they are my Adversaries; but I give myself unto Prayer.

And they have rewarded me Evil for Good, and Hatred for my Love. *Psal.* cix. 3, 4, 5.

Seek not to be Judge, being not able to take away Iniquity; lest at any Time thou fear the Person of the Mighty, and lay a stumbling Block in the Way of thy Uprightness.

Offend not against the Multitude of a City, and then thou shalt not cast thyself down among the People.

Bind not one Sin upon another, for in one thou shalt not be unpunished. *Eccles.* vii. 6, 7, 8.

Non jam prima peto Mnestheus, neque vincere certo:
Quanquam O! sed superent, quibus hoc, Neptune, dedisti.[1]

---

1 I, Mnestheus, am not now seeking the first place, nor do I seek to be victorious: However O! may they win to whom you, Neptune, have granted it.
Virgil, *Aeneid*, 5

In this pamphlet, which appeared on 31 December 1724, (the last to be published during the campaign against Wood), the Drapier addresses a radical Irish Whig who had always defended the country's right to legislative independence. The most relaxed, and least technical, of the *Letters*, it centres on the issue of the responsibility of the patriotic writer as a citizen. Of special interest is the 'Directions to the Printer', in which Swift disclaims any legal liability on the Drapier's part for contentious passages, and reveals his methods for concealing the identity of the author.

Directions to the Printer

Mr. *Harding,*

WHEN I sent you my former Papers, I cannot say I intended you either *Good* or *Hurt*; and yet you have happened through my Means to receive *both*. I pray God deliver you from any more of the *Latter*, and increase the *Former*. Your Trade, particularly in this Kingdom, is of all others, the most unfortunately circumstantiated; for, as you deal in the most worthless Kind of Trash; the Penny Productions of pennyless Scriblers; so, you often venture your Liberty, and sometimes your Lives, for the Purchase of half a Crown; and, by your own Ignorance, are punished for other Men's Actions.

I am afraid you, in particular, think you have Reason to complain of me, for your own, and your Wife's Confinement in Prison, to your great Expence as well as Hardship; and for a Prosecution still impending. But I will tell you, Mr. *Harding*, how that Matter standeth. Since the Press hath lain under so strict an Inspection, those who have a Mind to inform the World are become so cautious, as to keep themselves, if possible, out of the Way of Danger. My Custom, therefore, is to dictate to an Apprentice who can write in a feigned Hand; and, what is written we send to your House by a Black-guard Boy. But, at the same Time, I do assure you, upon my Reputation, that I never did send you any Thing, for which I thought you could possibly be called to an Account. And you will be my Witness, that I always desired you, by a Letter, to take some good Advice before you ventured to print; because I knew the *Dexterity* of *Dealers in the Law*, at finding out something to fasten on, where no Evil is meant. I am told, indeed, that you did accordingly consult several very able Persons; and even *some*, who afterwards *appeared against you*: To which I can only answer, that you must either change your *Advisers*, or determine to print nothing that comes from a *Drapier*.

I desire you will send the inclosed Letter, directed to my Lord Viscount *Molesworth*, at his House at *Brackdenstown* near *Swords*: But I would have it sent *printed*, for the Convenience of his Lordship's Reading; because this counterfeit Hand of my Apprentice is not very legible. And if you think fit to publish it, I would have you first get it read over carefully by some *notable* Lawyer: I am assured, you will find enough of them who are Friends to the *Drapier*, and will do it without a Fee; which, I am afraid, you can ill afford after all your Expences. For, although I have taken so much Care, that I think it impossible to find a Topick out of the following Papers for sending you again to Prison; yet I will not venture to be your Guarantee.

This ensuing Letter containeth only a short Account of myself, and an humble Apology for my former Pamphlets, especially the *last*; with little mention of Mr. *Wood* or his *Halfpence*, because I have already said enough upon that Subject, until Occasion shall be given for *new Fears*; and, in that Case, you may perhaps hear from me again.

I am, your Friend and Servant,

M. B.

From my Shop in
St. *Francis-street,*
Dec. 14, 1724.

P.S. For want of Intercourse between you and me, which I never will suffer, your People are apt to make very gross Errors in the Press, which I desire you will provide against.

Right Honourable * Lord Viscount *Molesworth*, at his House at *Brackdenstown*, near *Swords*.

My Lord,

I REFLECT too late on the Maxim of common Observers, that those, who meddle in Matters out of their Calling, will have Reason to repent; which is now verified in me: For, by engaging in the Trade of a Writer, I have drawn upon myself the Displeasure of the Government, signified by a *Proclamation*; promising a Reward of three hundred Pounds, to the first *faithful* Subject who shall be able, and inclined to *inform* against me. To which I may add the *laudable Zeal and Industry* of my Lord Chief-Justice *Whitshed*, in his Endeavours to discover so dangerous a Person. Therefore, whether I repent or no, I have certainly Cause to do so; and the common Observation still standeth good.

It will sometimes happen, I know not how, in the Course of human Affairs, that a Man shall be made liable to *legal* Animadversions, where he hath nothing to answer for, either to *God* or his *Country*; and condemned at *Westminster-hall*, for what he will never be charged with at the *Day of Judgment*.

After strictly examining my own Heart, and consulting some Divines of great Reputation, I cannot accuse myself of any ** *Malice or Wickedness against the Publick; of any Design to sow Sedition; of reflecting on the King and his Ministers; or of endeavouring to alienate the Affections of the People of this Kingdom from those of* England. All I can charge myself with is, a weak Attempt to serve a Nation in Danger of Destruction, by a most wicked and malicious Projector; without waiting until I were called to its Assistance: Which Attempt, however it may perhaps give me the Title of *Pragmatical and Overweening*, will never lie a Burthen upon my Conscience. God knows, whether I may not with all my Caution have already run

---

* *Robert Molesworth*, created Lord Viscount *Molesworth* of *Swords* in the County of *Dublin*, and Baron of *Philipstown* in the *King's* County, the 16th of *July* 1716, 2 George I. This Nobleman wrote an Account of *Denmark*, being Envoy Extraordinary from *England* to that Court in the Year 1692. His Lordship was born in *Dublin*, and educated in that University.
** Articles mentioned in the Indictment, and *vide* the proclamation.

myself into a second Danger, by offering thus much in my own Vindication. For I have heard of a *Judge*, who, upon the Criminal's
Appeal to the *dreadful Day of Judgment*, told him, he had incurred
a *Premunire* for *appealing to a foreign Judisdiction:* And of another
in *Wales*, who severely checked the Prisoner for offering the same
Plea; taxing him with reflecting on the Court by such a Comparison;
because *Comparisons were odious.*

But, in order to make some Excuse for being more speculative than
others of my Condition, I desire your Lordship's Pardon while I am
doing a very foolish Thing; which is to give you some little Account
of myself.

I was bred at a Free-School, where I acquired some little
Knowledge in the *Latin Tongue.*[2] I served my Apprenticeship in
London, and there set up for myself with good Success, until, by
the *Death of some Friends, and the Misfortunes of others*, I
returned into this Kingdom; and began to employ my Thoughts in
cultivating the *Woollen-Manufacture* through all its Branches;
wherein I met with great Discouragement, and powerful Opposers;
whose Objections appeared to me very strange and singular. They
argued, that the People of *England* would be offended, if our
Manufactures were brought to equal theirs: And even some of the
Weaving Trade were my Enemies; which I could not but look upon
as *absurd* and *unnatural*. I remember your Lordship, at that
Time, did me the Honour to come into my Shop, where I shewed
you a Piece * of *Black and White Stuff*, just sent from the
Dyer; which you were pleased to approve of, and be my Customer
for it.

However, I was so mortified, that I resolved, for the future, to
sit quietly in my Shop, and deal in *common Goods*, like the rest
of my Brethren; until it happened some Months ago, considering
with myself, that the *lower and poorer Sort of People* wanted a *plain,
strong, coarse Stuff, to defend them against cold* Easterly *Winds,
which then blew very fierce and blasting for a long Time together*;
I contrived one on purpose, which sold very well all over the
Kingdom, and preserved many thousands from *Agues*. I then made
a ** *second* and a *third* Kind of *Stuffs* for the *Gentry*, with the same
Success; Insomuch, that an *Ague* hath hardly been heard of for some
Time.

---

  * By this meant, a preceding Discourse in this Volume, entitled, *a proposal for the
  Universal Use of Irish Manufactures.*
  ** Alluding to the *Drapier's* three first Letters.
  2 What follows is an extended, and transparent, allegory of Swift's own career, as
  the original annotations by him make clear.

This incited me so far, that I ventured upon a * *fourth* Piece, made of the best *Irish* Wool I could get, and I thought it grave and rich enough to be worn by the best *Lord* or *Judge* of the Land; But, of late, some *great Folks* complain, as I hear, that, when they had it on, they felt a *Shuddering in their Limbs*, and have thrown it off in a Rage; cursing to Hell the poor *Drapier*, who invented it: So that I am determined never to *work for Persons of Quality* again, except for your *Lordship* and a *very few more*.

I assure your Lordship, upon the Word of an honest Citizen, that I am not richer, by the Value of one of Mr. *Wood's* Halfpence, with the Sale of all the several *Stuffs* I have contrived: For I give the whole Profit to the *Dyers* and *Pressers*. And, therefore, I hope you will please to believe, that no other Motive, besides the Love of my Country, could engage me to busy my Head and Hands, to the Loss of my Time, and the Gain of nothing but *Vexation* and *ill Will*.

I have now in Hand one *Piece of Stuff* to be woven on purpose for your Lordship; although I might be ashamed to offer it to you, after I have confessed, that it will be made only from the ** *Shreds and Remnants of the Wool employed in the Former*. However, *I shall work* it up as well as I can; and at worst, you need only give it among your Tenants.

I am very sensible how ill your Lordship is like to be entertained with the Pedantry of a *Drapier*, in the Terms of his own Trade. How will the Matter be mended, when you find me entering again, although very sparingly, into an Affair of State? For such is now grown the Controversy with Mr. *Wood*, if some *great Lawyers* are to be credited. And as it often happens at Play, that Men begin with *Farthings*, and go on to *Gold*, until some of them lose their Estates and die in Jayl; so it may possibly fall out in my Case, that, by *playing* too long with Mr. *Wood's* Halfpence, I may be drawn in to pay a *Fine*, double to the Reward for *Betraying* me; be sent to Prison, and *not be delivered thence until I have paid the uttermost Farthing*.

There are, My Lord, three Sorts of Persons with whom I am resolved never to dispute; A *Highwayman* with a Pistol at my Breast; *a Troop of Dragoons* who come to plunder my House; and a *Man of the Law* who can make a Merit of accusing me. In each of these Cases, *which are almost the same*, the best Method is to *keep out of the Way*; and the next best is to *deliver your Money, surrender your House, and confess nothing*.

I am told, that the two Points in my last Letter, from which an Occasion of Offence hath been taken, are, where I mention His

---

* Meaning the fourth Letter, against which the Proclamation was issued.
** Meaning the present Letter.

Majesty's Answer to the Address of the House of Lords upon Mr. *Wood's* Patent; and where I discourse upon *Ireland's* being a *Dependent Kingdom*. As to the former, I can only say, that I have treated it with the utmost Respect and Caution; and I thought it necessary to shew where *Wood's* Patent differed, in many essential Parts, from all others that ever had been granted, because, the contrary had, for want of due Information, been so strongly and so largely asserted. As to the other, of *Ireland's Dependency*; I confess to have often heard it mentioned, but was never able to understand what it meant. This gave me the Curiosity to enquire among several eminent Lawyers, who professed they knew nothing of the Matter. I then turned over all the Statutes of both Kingdoms without the least Information, further than an *Irish* Act that I quoted of the 33d Year of *Henry* VIII. uniting *Ireland* to *England* under one King.[3] I cannot say I was *sorry* to be disappointed in my Search; because it is certain, I could be *contented to depend only* upon *God* and my *Prince*, and the *Laws of my own Country, after the Manner of other Nations*. But since my *Betters* are of a *different Opinion*, and desire *further Dependencies*, I shall outwardly submit; yet still insisting in my own Heart, upon the *Exception* I made of M. *B. Drapier:* Indeed that Hint was borrowed from an idle Story I had heard in *England:* which perhaps may be common and beaten; but, because it *insinuates neither Treason nor Sedition*, I will just barely relate it.

Some Hundred Years ago, when the Peers were so great, that the Commons were looked upon as little better than their *Dependents*; a Bill was brought in for making some new Additions to the Power and Privileges of the Peerage. After it was read, one Mr. *Drue*,[4] a Member of the House, stood up, and said he very much approved the Bill, and would give his Vote to have it pass; but however, for some Reasons best known to himself, he desired that a Clause might be inserted for *excepting the Family of the* Drues. The Oddness of the Proposition taught others to reflect a little; and the Bill was thrown out.

Whether I were mistaken, or *went too far* in examining the *Dependency*, must be left to the impartial Judgment of the World, as well as to the Courts of Judicature; although indeed not in so *effectual* and *decisive* a Manner. But to affirm, as I hear some do, in order to countenance a fearful and servile Spirit, that this Point did

---

3 A point central to the previous pamphlet, *To the Whole People of Ireland*, in which the Drapier had rejected the suggestion that Ireland is constitutionally 'dependent' on England. He continued to insist that both countries simply, and willingly, shared the same monarch.

4 Probably Edward Drew (1542–1598), Judge and later M.P. for London, with a reputation for witty and rhetorical speeches.

not *belong to my Subject*, is a false and foolish Objection. There were several scandalous Reports industriously spread by *Wood* and his Accomplices to discourage all Opposition against his infamous Project. They gave it out that we were prepared for a *Rebellion*; and that we disputed the King's *Prerogative*; and were shaking off our *Dependency*. The first went so far, and obtained so much Belief against the most visible Demonstrations to the contrary, that a great Person of this Kingdom, now in *England*, sent over such an Account of it to his Friends, as would make any good Subject both grieve and tremble. I thought it therefore necessary to treat that Calumny as it deserved. Then I proved by an invincible Argument, that we could have no Intention to dispute His Majesty's *Prerogative*; because the *Prerogative* was not concerned in the Question; the Civilians and Lawyers of all Nations agreeing, that *Copper is not Money*. And lastly, to clear us from the Imputation of shaking off our *Dependency*, I shewed wherein I thought, and shall ever think, this *Dependency* consisted; and cited the Statute above-mentioned, made in *Ireland*; by which it is enacted, that *whoever is King of England shall be King of* Ireland; and that the two Kingdoms shall be *for ever knit together under one King*. This, as I conceived, did wholly acquit us of intending to break our *Dependency*; because it was altogether out of our Power: For surely no King of *England* will ever consent to the Repeal of this Statute.

But upon this Article I am charged with a heavier Accusation. It is said that I *went too far*, when I declared, that *if ever the* Pretender *should come to be fixed on the Throne of* England *(which God forbid) I would so far venture to transgress this Statute, that I would lose the last Drop of my Blood, before I would submit to him as* King *of* Ireland.

This, I hear on all Sides, is the strongest and weightiest Objection against me; and which hath given the most Offence; that I should be so bold to declare against a direct Statute; and that any Motive, how strong soever, could make me reject a King, whom *England* should receive. Now, if, in defending myself from this Accusation, I should freely confess, that I *went too far*; that the Expression was very indiscreet, although occasioned by my Zeal for his present Majesty, and His Protestant Line, in the House of *Hanover*; that I shall be careful never to offend again in the like Kind; and that I hope this free Acknowledgment and Sorrow for my Error will be some Attonement, and a little soften the Hearts of my powerful Adversaries: I say, if I should offer such a Defence as this, I do not doubt, but the People would wrest it to an ill Meaning, by a spiteful Interpretation. And therefore, since I cannot think of any other Answer which that Paragraph can admit, I will leave it to the Mercy of every candid Reader; but still without recanting my own Opinion.

I will now venture to tell your Lordship a Secret, wherein I fear you are too deeply concerned. You will therefore please to know, that this Habit of writing and discoursing, wherein I unfortunately differ from *almost* the whole Kingdom, and am apt to grate the Ears of more than I could wish, was acquired during my Apprenticeship in *London*, and a long Residence there after I had set up for myself. Upon my Return and Settlement here, I thought I had only *changed one Country of Freedom for another*. I had been long conversing with the Writings of your Lordship, Mr. *Locke*, Mr. *Molineaux*, Colonel *Sidney*, and other dangerous Authors,[5] who talk of 'Liberty as a Blessing, to which the whole Race of Mankind hath an Original Title; whereof nothing but unlawful Force can divert them,' I knew a good deal of the several *Gothick*[6] Institutions in *Europe*; and by what Incidents and Events they came to be destroyed: And I ever thought it the most uncontrolled and universally agreed Maxim, that 'Freedom consisteth in a People being governed by Laws made with their own Consent; and Slavery in the contrary;' I have been likewise told, and believe it to be true; that *Liberty* and *Property* are Words of known Use and Signification in this Kingdom; and the very Lawyers pretend to understand, and have them often in their Mouths. These were the Errors which have misled me; and to which alone I must impute the severe Treatment I have received. But I shall in Time *grow wiser*, and learn to consider my *Driver*, the *Road I am in*, and *with whom I am yoked*. This I will venture to say; that the boldest and most obnoxious Words, I ever delivered, would in *England* have only exposed me as a stupid Fool, who went to prove that 'the Sun shone in a clear Summer's Day:' And I have Witnesses ready to depose, that your Lordship hath said and writ fifty Times worse; and, what is still an Aggravation, with infinitely more Wit and Learning, and stronger Arguments: So that, as Politicks run,

5 In 1723 Molesworth had written a pamphlet, *Considerations for Promoting Agriculture*, which Swift had warmly praised. John Locke (1632–1704), political philosopher, author of *Two Treatises on Civil Government* (1690), written partly to legitimise the 'Glorious Revolution'. These *Treatises*, a most important influence on the Drapier's arguments, denounced absolute monarchy and encouraged the principle of 'contractual government'. For Molyneux, friend and correspondent of Locke, see n.7 to *The Whole People of Ireland*. Colonel Algernon Sidney (1622–83), Republican officer during the Cromwellian campaign in Ireland; after the Restoration, executed for plotting against the King. Author of *Discourses concerning Government*, first published in 1698, which attacked absolutism and defended the supreme rights of parliament. As a 'fanatic', Sidney seems an uncharacteristic type for the Drapier's case.

6 In the sense of 'mediaeval'.

I do not know a Person of more exceptionable Principles than yourself: And, if ever I shall be discovered, I think you will be bound in Honour to pay my Fine, and support me in Prison; or else I may chance to *inform* against you by Way of *Reprisal.*

In the mean Time, I beg your Lordship to receive my Confession; that if there be any such Thing as a *Dependency* of *Ireland* upon *England,* otherwise than as I have explained it, either by the *Law* of *God,* of *Nature,* of *Reason,* of *Nations,* or of the *Land* (which I shall die rather than grant) then was the *Proclamation* against me the most *Merciful* that ever was put out; and instead of accusing me as *Malicious, Wicked,* and *Seditious;* it might have been directly as guilty of *High-Treason.*

All I desire is, that the Cause of my Country against Mr. *Wood* may not suffer by any Inadvertency of mine: Whether *Ireland* dependeth upon *England,* or only upon *God,* the *King,* and the *Law;* I hope no Man will assert that it *dependeth* upon Mr. *Wood.* I should be heartily sorry, that this *commendable* Resentment against me should accidentally (and I *hope* what was never intended) strike a Damp upon that Spirit in all Ranks and Corporations of Men against the desparate and ruinous Designs of Mr. *Wood.* Let my Countrymen blot out those Parts in my last Letter which they dislike; and let no *Rust remain* in my *Sword,* to cure the Wounds I have given to our most mortal Enemy. When Sir *Charles Sidley*[7] was taking the Oaths, where several Things were to be *Renounced;* he said, he loved *Renouncing;* asked if any more were to be *Renounced;* for he was ready to *Renounce* as much as they pleased. Although I am not so thorough a *Renouncer;* yet let me have but *Good City Security* against this pestilent Coinage, and I shall be ready not only to *renounce* every Syllable in all my four Letters, but deliver them chearfully with my own *Hands* into *those* of the common *Hangman,* to be burnt with no better Company than the *Coiner's Effigies,* if any Part of it hath escaped out of the *Secular Hands* of my faithful Friends the common People.

But, whatever the Sentiments of *some People* may be, I think it is agreed, that many of those who *subscribed* against me, are on the Side of a vast Majority in the Kingdom, who opposed Mr. *Wood:* And it was with great Satisfaction, that I observed some *Right Honourable Names* very *amicably* joined with my own at the Bottom of a *strong Declaration* against him and his Coin. But if

---

7 Sir Charles Sidley (1639–1701), notorious parliamentary wit and literary dilletante. Author of several pamphlets on the Williamite revolution, which he accepted reluctantly. A close friend of Dryden, who was a cousin of Swift on the mother's side.

the Admission of it among us be *already determined*, the *worthy Person*, who is to *betray* me, ought in Prudence to do it with all convenient Speed; or else it may be difficult to find three hundred Pounds in *Sterling* for the Discharge of his *Hire*; when the Publick shall have lost five hundred thousand, if there be so much in the Nation; besides four fifths of its annual Income for ever.

I am told by Lawyers, that in Quarrels between Man and Man it is of much Weight which of them gave the first Provocation, or struck the first Blow. It is manifest that Mr. *Wood* hath done both: And therefore I should humbly propose to have him first *hanged*, and his *Dross* thrown into the Sea: After which the *Drapier* will be ready to stand his Trial. 'It must needs be that Offences come; but Woe unto him by whom the Offence cometh.'[8] If Mr. *Wood* had held his *Hand*, every body else would have held their *Tongues*: And then there would have been little Need of *Pamphlets, Juries*, or *Proclamations* upon this Occasion. The Provocation must needs have been very great, which could stir up an obscure, indolent *Drapier* to become an *Author*. One would almost think, the very *Stones* in the Street would *rise* up in such a Cause: And I am not sure, they will not *do so* against Mr. *Wood*, if ever he comes within their Reach. It is a known Story of the dumb Boy, whose Tongue forced a Passage for Speech by the Horror of seeing a Dagger at his Father's Throat. This may lessen the Wonder, that a Tradesman, hid in Privacy and Silence, should *cry out* when the Life and Being of his political *Mother* are attempted before his Face; and by so infamous a Hand.

But, in the mean Time, Mr. *Wood*, the *Destroyer* of a Kingdom, walks about in Triumph (unless it be true, that he is in Jayl for Debt) while he, who endeavoured to *assert the Liberty of his Country*, is forced to *hide his Head* for occasionally dealing in a Matter of *Controversy*. However, I am not the first who hath been condemned to Death for *gaining a great Victory* over a powerful Enemy, by disobeying for *once* the strict Orders of Military Discipline.

I am now resolved to follow (after the usual Proceeding of Mankind, because it is too late) the Advice given me by a certain *Dean*.* He shewed me the Mistake I was in of trusting to the general good Will of the People; that I had succeeded hitherto better than could be expected; but that some *unfortunate circumstantial Lapse* would probably bring me within the Reach of *Power*: That my good Intentions would be no Security against 'those who watched every Motion of my Pen in the Bitterness of my Soul'. He produced an Instance of a Person as innocent, as disinterested, and as well

* The Author, it is supposed, meaneth himself.
8 Matthew 18.7.

meaning as myself; who had written a * very seasonable and in-
offensive Treatise, exhorting the People of this Kingdom to wear their
own Manufactures; for which, however, the Printer was persecuted
with the utmost Virulence; *the Jury sent back nine Times*; and the
Man given up to the Mercy of the Court. The Dean further observed,
That I was in a Manner left alone to stand the *Battle*; while others,
who had ten thousand Times better Talents than a *Drapier*, were
so prudent to lie still; and perhaps thought it no unpleasant Amusement, to look on with Safety, while another was giving them such
Diversion, at the Hazard of his Liberty and Fortune; and thought
they made a sufficient Recompence by a little Applause: whereupon
he concluded with a short Story of a *Jew* at *Madrid*; who being condemned to the Fire on Account of his Religion, a Croud of School-
boys followed him to the Stake, and apprehending they might lose
their *Sport*, if he should happen to recant, would often *clap him on
the Back*, and cry, *Sta firmo Moyese (Moses continue stedfast.)*

I allow this Gentleman's Advice to have been very good, and his
Observations just; and in one Respect my Condition is worse than
that of the *Jew*, for *no Recantation will save me.* However it should
seem by *some late Proceedings*, that my State is not altogether
deplorable. This I can impute to nothing but the Steadiness of *two
impartial Grand Juries*; which hath confirmed in me an Opinion I
have long entertained; That, as Philosophers say, 'Virtue is seated
in the Middle;'[9] so in another Sense, the little *Virtue* left in the
World is chiefly to be found among the *middle* Rank of Mankind;
who are neither *allured* out of her Paths by *Ambition*, nor *driven*
by *Poverty*.

Since the *Proclamation*, occasioned by my last Letter, and a *due*
Preparation for Proceeding against me in a Court of Justice, there
have been two printed Papers clandestinely spread about; whereof
no Man is able to trace the Original, further than by *Conjecture*;
which, with its usual Charity, layeth them to my Account.[10] The
former is entitled, *Seasonable Advice*, and appeareth to have been
intended for Information of the Grand Jury, upon the Supposition
of a Bill to be prepared against that Letter. The other is an

---

* The Author meaneth himself again; in the Discourse advising the People of *Ireland*
to wear their own Manufactures.

9 A belief usually traced to Aristotle's *Ethics*.

10 The two named pieces which follow were written by Swift himself, immediately
after his printer, Harding, was arrested. *Seasonable Advice* asked the jury not
to find the printer or the pamphlet guilty of sedition, as both served a
patriotic cause. When Justice Whitshed dismissed the uncooperative jury, Swift
printed and circulated *An Extract*, details of seventeenth century legal
cases which proved the illegality of Whitshed's behaviour.

Extract from a printed Book of Parliamentary Proceedings, in the Year 1680; containing an angry Resolution of the House of Commons in *England*, against *dissolving Grand Juries*. As to the former, your Lordship will find it to be the Work of a more artful Hand, than that of a common *Drapier*. It hath been censured for endeavouring to influence the Minds of a Jury, which ought to be wholly free and unbiassed; and for that Reason, *it is manifest*, that no *Judge* was ever known, either *upon* or *off* the Bench, either by *himself*, or his *Dependents*, to use the *least Insinuation*, that might possibly affect the Passions, or Interests, of any one single *Jury-Man*, much less of a whole *Jury*; whereof every Man *must be convinced*, who will just give himself the Trouble to dip into the common printed Trials: So as it is amazing to think, what a Number of *upright Judges* there have been in both Kingdoms, for above *sixty Years past*; which, considering how long they held their Offices *during Pleasure*, as they *still do among us*, I account next to a *Miracle*.

As to the other Paper, I must confess it is a sharp Censure from an *English* House of Commons against *dissolving Grand Juries*, by any Judge before the End of the Term, Assizes, or Sessions, while Matters are under their Consideration; and not presented as arbitrary, illegal, destructive to publick Justice, a manifest Violation of his Oath, and is a Means to subvert the fundamental Laws of the Kingdom.

However, the Publisher seemeth to have been mistaken in what he aimed at. For, whatever *Dependence* there may be of *Ireland* upon *England*; I hope he would not insinuate, that the Proceedings of a Lord Chief-Justice in *Ireland* must *depend* upon a *Resolution* of an *England* House of Commons. Besides, that *Resolution*, although it were levelled against a particular Lord Chief-Justice, Sir *William Scroggs*, yet the Occasion was directly contrary. For, *Scroggs dissolved the* Grand Jury of *London*, for fear they *should* present; but ours in *Dublin* was *dissolved*, because they would *not* present, which *wonderfully alters the Case*. And, therefore, a *second* Grand Jury supplied that Defect by making a Presentment that hath *pleased the whole Kingdom*. However, I think it is agreed by all Parties, that both the one and the other *Jury* behaved themselves in such a Manner, as ought to be remembered to their Honour, while there shall be any Regard left among us for *Virtue* or *Publick Spirit*.

I am confident, your Lordship will be of my Sentiments in one Thing; that some short, plain, authentick Tract might be published for the Information both of *Petty* and *Grand Juries*, how far their Power reacheth, and where it is limited; and that a printed Copy of such a Treatise might be deposited in every Court, to be consulted by the Jurymen, before they consider of their Verdict; by which Abundance of Inconveniencies would be avoided; whereof innumerable Instances might be produced from former Times, because I will say nothing of the present.

I have read somewhere of an *Eastern* King, who put a Judge to Death for an iniquitous Sentence; and ordered his *Hide to be stuffed into a Cushion*, and placed upon the Tribunal for the Son to sit on; who was preferred to his Father's Office. I fancy, such a Memorial might not have been unuseful to a Son of Sir *William Scroggs*, and that both he and his Successors would often *wriggle* in their Seats, as long as the Cushion lasted: I wish the Relater had told us what Number of such *Cushions* there might be in that Country.

I cannot but observe to your Lordship, how nice and dangerous a Point it is grown, for a private Person to inform the People, even in an Affair, where the publick Interest and Safety are so highly concerned, as that of Mr. *Wood*; and this in a Country, where *Loyalty is woven into the very Hearts of the People*, seemeth a little extraordinary. Sir *William Scroggs* was the first who introduced that *commendable Acuteness in the Courts of Judicature*; but how far this Practice hath been imitated by his Successors, or *strained* upon Occasion, is out of my Knowledge. When Pamphlets unpleasing to the Ministry were presented as Libels, he would order the offensive Paragraphs to be read before him; and said it was strange, that the Judges and Lawyers of the King's-Bench should be duller than all the People of *England:* And he was often so very happy in applying the initial Letters of Names, and expounding dubious Hints, (the two common Expedients among Writers of that Class for escaping the Law) that he discovered much *more* than ever the Authors intended; as many of them, or their Printers, found to their Cost. If such Methods are to be followed in examining what I have already written, or may write hereafter, upon the Subject of Mr. *Wood*, I defy any Man of fifty Times my Understanding and Caution to avoid being entrapped; unless he will be content to write what none will read, by repeating over the old Arguments and Computations; whereof the World is already grown weary. So that my good Friend *Harding* lieth under this *Dilemma*; either to let my *learned Works* hang for ever drying upon his Lines; or venture to publish them at the Hazard of being laid by the Heels.

I need not tell your Lordship where the Difficulty lieth; It is true, that the King and the Laws *permit* us to refuse this Coin of Mr. *Wood*; but, at the same Time, it is equally true, that the King and the Laws *permit* us to receive it. Now, it is *barely* possible that the

Ministers in *England* may not suppose the Consequences of uttering that Brass among us to be so ruinous as we apprehend; because, perhaps, if they understand it in that Light, they would, in common Humanity, use their Credit with His Majesty for saving a *most loyal Kingdom from Destruction*. But, as long as it shall please those great Persons to think that Coin will not be so very pernicious to us, we lie under the Disadvantage of being censured as *obstinate* in not complying with a Royal Patent. Therefore, nothing remaineth, but to make Use of that *Liberty*, which the *King* and the *Laws* have left us, by continuing to refuse this Coin; and by frequent Remembrances to keep up that Spirit raised amongst us; which, otherwise, may be apt to flag, and perhaps in Time to sink altogether. For any publick Order against receiving or uttering Mr. *Wood's* Halfpence is not *reasonably* to be expected in this Kingdom, without Directions from *England*; which I think no body presumeth, or is so sanguine to hope.

But to confess the Truth, my Lord, I begin to grow weary of my Office as a Writer; and could heartily wish it were devolved upon my *Brethren*, the Makers of *Songs* and *Ballads*; who, perhaps, are the best qualified at present to gather up the Gleanings of this Controversy. As to myself, it hath been my Misfortune to begin, and pursue it upon a very wrong Foundation. For, having detected the Frauds and Falshoods of this vile Impostor *Wood*, in every Part, I foolishly *disdained* to have Recourse to *Whining*, *Lamenting*, and *Crying for Mercy*; but rather chose to appeal to *Law*, and *Liberty*, and *the common Rights of Mankind*, without considering the *Climate* I was in.

Since your last Residence in *Ireland*, I frequently have taken my Nag to ride about your Grounds; where I fancied myself to feel an Air of *Freedom* breathing round me; and I am glad the low Condition of a Tradesman did not qualify me to wait on you at your House; for then, I am afraid, my Writings would not have escaped *severer Censures*. But I have lately sold my Nag, and honestly told his greatest Fault, which was that of snuffing up the Air about *Brackdenstown*; whereby he became such a Lover of *Liberty*, that I could scarce hold him in. I have likewise buried, at the Bottom of a strong Chest, your Lordship's Writings, under a Heap of others that treat of *Liberty*; and spread over a *Layer* or two of *Hobbs, Filmer, Bodin,*[11] and many other Authors of

---

11 These three names are to be understood as defenders of absolutism and enemies of freedom. Thomas Hobbes (1588–1679), author of *Leviathan* (1651), often interpreted as justification of the omnipotent state. Sir Robert Filmer (d.1653), fervent Royalist whose *Patriarcha* was republished by later generations of Tories and Jacobites. Locke's *Treatises* repeatedly attacked Filmer's absolutism. Jean Bodin (1530–1596), French political theorist, author of *Le République*, translated in London in 1606. Defender of absolute sovereignty and divine right of monarchy.

that stamp, to be readiest at Hand, whenever I shall be disposed to take up a *new Set* of Principles in Government. In the mean Time, I design quietly to look to my Shop, and keep as far out of your Lordship's Influence as possible: And if you ever see any more of my Writings on this Subject, I promise you shall find them as innocent, as insipid, and without a Sting, as what I have now offered you. But, if your Lordship will please to give me an easy Lease of some Part of your Estate in *Yorkshire*, thither I will carry my Chest; and turning it upside down, resume my political Reading where I left it off; feed on plain, homely Fare, and live and die a *Free*, honest *English* Farmer: But not without Regret, for leaving my Countrymen under the Dread of the Brazen Talons of Mr. *Wood*; my most Loyal and Innocent Countrymen; to whom I owe so much for their good Opinion of me, and my poor Endeavours to serve them. I am, with the greatest Respect,

> *My Lord,*
> *Your Lordship's*
> *Most Obedient,*
> *And most Humble Servant,*

M. B.

From my Shop in
 St. *Francis-street,*
 Dec. 14, 1724.

A
Short VIEW
OF THE
STATE of *IRELAND*.

Written in the Year 1727

The *Short View* appeared, anonymously, on 19 March 1728, two months after the death of Stella, Swift's closest friend. It is the first in a series of bitterly pessimistic pamphlets on Ireland's distorted economy. The triumph and optimism of *The Drapier's Letters* were short-lived, since Ireland's economic and political situation remained unchanged. In 1729, *A Short View* was reprinted as No. 15 of the *Intelligencer*, a periodical set up by Swift and Thomas Sheridan, his clerical friend from Co. Cavan, grandfather of the dramatist, Richard Brinsley Sheridan.

A
Short VIEW

OF THE

STATE of *IRELAND*.

Written in the Year 1727

I AM assured, that it hath, for some Time, been practised as a Method of making Men's Court, when they are asked about the Rate of Lands, the Abilities of Tenants, the State of Trade and Manufacture in this Kingdom, and how their Rents are paid; to answer, that in their Neighbourhood, all Things are in a flourishing Condition, the Rent and Purchase of Land every Day encreasing. And if a Gentleman happen to be a little more sincere in his Representations; besides being looked on as not well affected, he is sure to have a Dozen Contradictors at his Elbow. I think it is no Manner of Secret, why these Questions are so *cordially* asked, or so *obligingly* answered.

But since, with regard to the Affairs of this Kingdom, I have been using all Endeavours to subdue my Indignation; to which, indeed, I am not provoked by any personal Interest, being not the Owner of one Spot of Ground in the whole *Island*; I shall only enumerate by Rules generally known, and never contradicted, what are the true Causes of any Countries flourishing and growing rich; and then examine what Effects arise from those Causes in the Kingdom of *Ireland*.

The first Cause of a Kingdom's thriving, is the Fruitfulness of the Soil, to produce the Necessaries and Conveniencies of Life; not only sufficient for the Inhabitants, but for Exportation into other Countries.

The Second, is the Industry of the People, in working up all their native Commodities, to the last Degree of Manufacture.

The Third, is the Conveniency of safe Ports and Havens, to carry out their own Goods, as much manufactured, and bring in those of others, as little manufactured, as the Nature of mutual Commerce will allow.

The Fourth is, that the Natives should, as much as possible, export and import their Goods in Vessels of their own Timber, made in their own Country.

The Fifth, is the Priviledge of a free Trade in all foreign Countries, which will permit them; except to those who are in War with their own Prince or State.

The Sixth, is, by being governed only by Laws made with their own Consent; for otherwise they are not a free People. And therefore, all Appeals for Justice, or Applications for Favour or Preferment, to another Country, are so many grievous Impoverishments.

The Seventh is, by Improvement of Land, Encouragement of Agriculture, and thereby encreasing the Number of their People; without which, any Country, however blessed by Nature, must continue poor.

The Eighth, is the Residence of the Prince, or chief Administrator of the Civil Power.

The Ninth, is the Concourse of Foreigners for Education, Curiosity, or Pleasure; or as to a general Mart of Trade.

The Tenth, is by disposing all Offices of Honour, Profit, or Trust, only to the Natives, or at least with very few Exceptions; where Strangers have long inhabited the Country, and are supposed to understand, and regard the Interest of it as their own.

The Eleventh, is when the Rents of Lands, and Profits of Employments, are spent in the Country which produced them, and not in another; the former of which will certainly happen, where the Love of our native Country prevails.

The Twelfth, is by the publick Revennes being all spent and employed at home; except on the Occasions of a foreign War.

The Thirteenth is, where the People are not obliged, unless they find it for their own Interest or Conveniency, to receive any Monies, except of their own Coinage by a publick Mint, after the Manner of all civilized Nations.

The Fourteenth, is a Disposition of the People of a Country to wear their own Manufactures, and import as few Incitements to Luxury, either in Cloaths, Furniture, Food, or Drink, as they possibly can live conveniently without.

There are many other Causes of a Nation's thriving, which I cannot at present recollect; but without Advantage from at least some of these: After turning my Thoughts a long Time, I am not able to discover from whence our Wealth proceeds, and therefore would gladly be better informed. In the mean Time, I will here examine what Share falls to *Ireland* of these Causes, or of the Effects and Consequences.

It is not my Intention to complain, but barely to relate Facts; and the Matter is not of small Importance. For it is allowed, that a Man who lives in a solitary House, far from Help, is not wise in endeavouring to acquire, in the Neighbourhood, the Reputation of being rich; because those who come for Gold, will go off with Pewter and Brass, rather than return empty: And in the common Practice of the World, those who possess most Wealth, make the least Parade; which they leave to others, who have nothing else to bear them out, in shewing their Faces on the *Exchange*.

As to the first Cause of a Nation's Riches, being the Fertility of the Soil, as well as Temperature of Climate, we have no Reason to complain; for, although the Quantity of unprofitable Land in this Kingdom, reckoning Bogg, and Rock, and barren Mountain, be double in Proportion to what it is in *England*; yet the native Productions which both Kingdoms deal in, are very near on Equality in Point of Goodness; and might, with the same Encouragement, be as well manufactured. I except Mines and Minerals; in some of which, however, we are only defective in Point of Skill and Industry.

In the Second, which is the Industry of the People; our Misfortune is not altogether owing to our own Fault, but to a Million of Discouragements.

The Conveniency of Ports and Havens, which Nature hath bestowed so liberally on this Kingdom, is of no more Use to us, than a beautiful Prospect to a Man shut up in a Dungeon.

As to Shipping of its own, *Ireland* is so utterly unprovided, that of all the excellent Timber cut down within these Fifty or Sixty Years; it can hardly be said, that the Nation hath received the Benefit of one valuable House to dwell in, or one Ship to trade with.

IRELAND is the only Kingdom I ever heard or read of, either in ancient or modern Story, which was denied the Liberty of exporting their native Commodities and Manufactures, wherever they pleased; except to Countries at War with their own Prince or State: Yet this Privilege, by the Superiority of meer Power, is refused us, in the most momentous Parts of Commerce; besides an Act of Navigation,[1] to which we never consented, pinned down upon us, and rigorously executed; and a Thousand other unexampled Circumstances, as grievous, as they are invidious to mention. To go unto the rest.

It is too well known, that we are forced to obey some Laws we never consented to; which is a Condition I must not call by its true uncontroverted Name, for fear of Lord Chief Justice

---

1 A series of Navigation Acts in the 1660s prohibited Irish competition with English trade.

Whitshed's Ghost, with his * *Libertas & natale Solum*, written as
a Motto on his Coach, as it stood at the Door of the Court, while
he was perjuring himself to betray both.[2] Thus, we are in the Condition of Patients, who have Physick sent them by Doctors at a
Distance, Strangers to their Constitution, and the Nature of their
Disease: And thus, we are forced to pay five Hundred *per Cent* to
decide our properties; in all which, we have likewise the Honour
to be distinguished from the whole Race of Mankind.

As to Improvement of Land; those few who attempt that, or Planting, through Covetousness, or Want of Skill, generally leave Things
worse than they were; neither succeeding in Trees nor Hedges; and
by running into the Fancy of Grazing, after the Manner of the
Scythians,[3] are every Day depopulating the Country.

We are so far from having a King to reside among us, that even
the Viceroy is generally absent four Fifths of his Time in the
Government.

No Strangers from other Countries, make this a Part of their
Travels; where they can expect to see nothing, but Scenes of Misery
and Desolation.

Those who have the Misfortune to be born here, have the least
Title to any considerable Employment; to which they are seldom
preferred, but upon a political Consideration.

One third Part of the Rents of *Ireland*, is spent in *England*; which,
with the Profit of Employments, Pensions, Appeals, Journies of
Pleasure or Health, Education at the *Inns* of Court, and both Univer-
sities, Remittances at Pleasure, the Pay of all Superior Officers in
the Army; and other Incidents, will amount to a full half of the
Income of the whole Kingdom, all clear Profit to *England*.

We are denied the Liberty of Coining Gold, Silver, or even Copper. In the Isle of *Man*, they coin their own *Silver*; every petty Prince,
Vassal to the *Emperor*, can coin what Money he pleaseth. And in
this, as in most of the Articles already mentioned we are an Exception to all other States or Monarchies that were ever known in the
World.

As to the last, or Fourteenth Article, we take special Care to act
diametrically contrary to it in the whole Course of our Lives. Both
Sexes, but especially the Women, despise and abhor to wear any
of their own Manufactures, even those which are better made than

---

* *Liberty and my native Country.*

2 Lord Chief Justice Whitshed presided over the court cases involving Swift's 1720
   Proposal and the Drapier's *Letter to the Whole People of Ireland.* Swift vilified
   him at every opportunity.

3 An ancient nomadic tribe of Russian and Asiatic Europe.

in other Countries; particularly a Sort of Silk Plad, through which the Workmen are forced to run a Sort of Gold Thread that it may pass for *Indian*. Even Ale and Potatoes are imported from *England*, as well as Corn: And our foreign Trade is little more than Importation of *French* Wine; for which I am told we pay ready Money.

Now, if all this be true, upon which I could easily enlarge; I would be glad to know by what secret Method, it is, that we grow a rich and flourishing People, without *Liberty, Trade, Manufactures, Inhabitants, Money,* or the *Privilege of Coining;* without *Industry, Labour,* or *Improvement of Lands,* and with more than half the Rent and Profits of the whole *Kingdom,* annually exported; for which we receive not a single Farthing: And to make up all this, nothing worth mentioning, except the Linnen of the *North,* a Trade casual, corrupted, and at Mercy; and some Butter from *Cork.* If we do flourish, it must be against every Law of Nature and Reason; like the Thorn at *Glassenbury,* that blossoms in the Midst of Winter.[4]

Let the worthy *Commissioners* who come from *England,* ride round the Kingdom, and observe the Face of Nature, or the Faces of the Natives; the Improvement of the Land; the thriving numerous Plantations; the noble Woods; the Abundance and Vicinity of Country-Seats; the commodious Farmers Houses and Barns; the Towns and Villages, where every Body is busy, and thriving with all Kind of Manufactures; the Shops full of Goods, wrought to Perfection, and filled with Customers; the comfortable Diet and Dress, and Dwellings of the People; the vast Numbers of Ships in our Harbours and Docks, and Ship-wrights in our Seaport-Towns; the Roads crouded with Carriers, laden with rich Manufactures; the perpetual Concourse to and fro of pompous Equipages.

With what Envy, and Admiration, would those Gentlemen return from so delightful a Progress? What glorious Reports would they make, when they went back to *England?*

But my heart is too heavy to continue this Irony longer; for it is manifest, that whatever Stranger took such a Journey, would be apt to think himself travelling in *Lapland,* or *Ysland,* rather than in a Country so favoured by Nature as ours, both in Fruitfulness of Soil, and Temperature of Climate. The miserable Dress, and Dyet, and Dwelling of the People. The general Desolation in most Parts of the Kingdom. The old Seats of the Nobility and Gentry all in Ruins, and no new ones in their Stead. The Families of Farmers, who pay great Rents, living in Filth and Nastiness upon Buttermilk and

---

4 Glastonbury. Town in Somerset with many religious and folkloristic legends, one of which explains the phenomenon of the December-rose as a celebration of the birth of Christ.

Potatoes, without a Shoe or Stocking to their Feet; or a House so convenient as an *English* Hog-sty, to receive them. These, indeed, may be comfortable Sights to an *English* Spectator; who comes for a short Time, only *to learn the Language*, and returns back to his own Country, whither he finds all our Wealth transmitted.

Nostrâ miserià magna es.[5]

There is not one Argument used to prove the Riches of *Ireland*, which is not a logical Demonstration of its Poverty.[6] The Rise of our Rents, is squeezed out of the very Blood, and Vitals, and Cloaths, and Dwellings of the Tenants; who live worse than *English* Beggars. The Lowness of Interest, in all other Countries a Sign of Wealth, is in us a Proof of Misery; there being no Trade to employ any Borrower. Hence, alone, comes the Dearness of Land, since the Savers have no other Way to lay out their Money. Hence the Dearness of Necessaries for Life; because the Tenants cannot afford to pay such extravagant Rates for Land, (which they must take, or go a-begging) without raising the Price of Cattle, and of Corn, although themselves should live upon Chaff. Hence our encrease of Buildings in this City; because Workmen have nothing to do, but employ one another; and one Half of them are infallibly undone. Hence the daily Encrease of *Bankers*; who may be a necessary Evil in a trading Country, but so ruinous in ours; who, for their private Advantage, have sent away all our Silver, and one Third of our Gold; so that within three Years past, the running Cash of the Nation, which was about five Hundred Thousand Pounds, is now less than two; and must daily diminish, unless we have Liberty to coin, as well as that important Kingdom the Isle of *Man*; and the meanest Prince in the *German* Empire, as I before observed.

I have sometimes thought, that this Paradox of the Kingdom growing rich, is chiefly owing to those worthy Gentlemen the BANKERS; who, except some Custom-house Officers, Birds of Passage, oppressive thrifty 'Squires, and a few others who shall be nameless, are the only thriving People among us: And I have often wished, that a Law were enacted to hang up half a Dozen *Bankers* every Year; and thereby interpose at least some short Delay, to the further Ruin of *Ireland*.[7]

YE *are idle, ye are idle*, answered *Pharoah* to the *Israelites*,

---

5 Our misery is extreme.

6 Especially the maxim that 'People are the Riches of a Nation'.

7 For Swift, bankers, like political and religious theorists, promoted dangerous speculation. He had also lost money in the South Sea Bubble fiasco, an investment he bitterly regretted.

when they complained to *his Majesty*, that they were forced to make Bricks without Straw.[8]

ENGLAND enjoys every one of those Advantages for enriching a Nation, which I have above enumerated; and, into the Bargain, a good Million returned to them every Year, without Labour or Hazard, or one Farthing Value received on our Side. But how long we shall be able to continue the Payment, I am not under the least Concern. One Thing I know, that *when the Hen is starved to Death, there will no more Golden Eggs.*

I think it a little unhospitable, and others may call it a subtil Piece of Malice; that, because there may be a Dozen Families in this Town, able to entertain their *English* Friends in a generous Manner at their Tables; their Guests, upon their Return to *England*, shall report, that we wallow in Riches and Luxury.

Yet, I confess, I have known an Hospital, where all the Houshold Officers grew rich; while the Poor, for whose Sake it was built, were almost starving for want of Food and Raiment.

To conclude. If *Ireland* be a rich and flourishing Kingdom; its Wealth and Prosperity must be owing to certain Causes, that are yet concealed from the whole Race of Mankind; and the Effects are equally invisible. We need not wonder at Strangers, when they deliver such Paradoxes; but a Native and Inhabitant of this Kingdom, who gives the same Verdict, must be either ignorant to Stupidity; or a Man pleaser, at the Expence of all Honour, Conscience, and Truth.

8 Exodus 5:17.

The INTELLIGENCER, No. 19

Sic vos, non vobis velera fertis oves.

Written in the Year 1728

The Intelligencer was a small weekly-paper started in May 1728 by Swift and his friend, Thomas Sheridan, dealing with contemporary issues of economic, political and literary interest. In this contribution by Swift, where he poses as a northern landlord appealing to the patriotic experience of the Drapier, the alarming prospect of Protestant emigration to America is raised. Government mismanagement, it is argued, will eventually result in the weakening of a settlement it once encouraged. Swift chooses the north because of its substantial Protestant population and its special manufacturing skills, especially in linen: if these people, the better-off Protestants, are forced to leave, then the economic and political situation is grave indeed. Swift visited friends in the north of Ireland regularly, especially in Co. Armagh, and during the summer of this year stayed with the Achesons at Markethill.

N.B. *In the following Discourse, the* Author *personates a Country Gentleman in the North of* Ireland. *And this Letter is supposed as directed to the* Drapier.

Having, on the 12th *of* October *last, received a Letter, signed* Andrew Dealer, *and* Patrick Pennyless; *I believe the following* Paper, *just come to my Hands, will be a sufficient Answer to it.*

The INTELLIGENCER, No. 19

Sic vos, non vobis velera fertis oves.[1]

Written in the Year 1728

SIR,

I AM a Country Gentleman, and a Member of *Parliament*, with an Estate of about 1400 *l.* a Year; which, as a *Northern* Landlord, I receive from about two hundred Tenants: And my Lands having been let near twenty Years ago, the Rents, until very lately, were esteemed not to be above half Value; yet by the intolerable Scarcity of *Silver*, I lye under the greatest Difficulties in receiving them, as well as in paying my Labourers, or buying any Thing necessary for my Family from *Tradesmen*, who are not able to be long out of their *Money*. But the Sufferings of me, and those of my Rank, are Trifles in Comparison of what the meaner Sort undergo; such as the *Buyers* and *Sellers*, at *Fairs* and *Markets*; the *Shopkeepers* in every *Town*; the *Farmers* in general; all those who travel with *Fish, Poultry, Pedlary-Ware*; and other Conveniences to sell: But, more especially, *Handicraftsmen*, who work for us by the Day, and common Labourers whom I have already mentioned. Both these Kind of People I am forced to employ until

1 Thus being yourselves sheep, you carry wool, but not for yourselves. From Donatus's *Life of Virgil*.

their Wages amount to a *Double-Pistole*, or a *Moidore*,[2] (for we
hardly have any *Gold* of lower Value left us) to divide it among
themselves as they can: And this is generally done at an *Ale-House*
or *Brandy-Shop*; where, besides the Cost of getting *drunk*, (which
is usually the Case) they must pay *Ten-pence* or a *Shilling*, for
changeing their *Piece* into *Silver*, to some *Huckstering Fellow*, who
follows that *Trade*. But, what is infinitely worse, those poor Men,
for want of due Payment, are forced to take up their *Oatmeal*, and
other Necessaries of Life, at almost double Value; and consequently, are not able to discharge half their Score; especially under the
Scarceness of *Corn*, for two Years past; and the melancholly Dis-
appointment of the present *Crop*.

The Causes of this, and a thousand other Evils, are clear and manifest
to you, and all thinking Men; although hidden from the Vulgar: These
indeed complain of hard Times, the Dearth of Corn, the Want of
Money, the Badness of Seasons; that their Goods bear no Price, and
the Poor cannot find Work; but their weak Reasonings never carry
them to the Hatred and Contempt borne us by our Neighbours and
Brethren, without the least Grounds of Provocation, who rejoice at our
Sufferings, although sometimes to their own Disadvantage. They consider not the dead Weight upon every beneficial Branch of our Trade;
that half our Revenues are annually sent to *England*; with many other
Grievances peculiar to this unhappy Kingdom, which keep us from
enjoying the common Benefits of Mankind; as you and some other
Lovers of their Country have so often observed, with such good
Inclinations, and so little Effect.

It is true indeed, that under our Circumstances, in general; this Complaint for the Want of *Silver*, may appear as ridiculous, as for a Man
to be impatient about a *cut Finger*, when he is struck with the *Plague*:
And yet a poor Fellow going to the *Gallows*, may be allowed to feel the
Smart of *Wasps* while he is upon *Tyburn-Road*. This Misfortune is so
urging, and vexatious in every Kind of small Traffick, and so hourly
pressing upon all Persons in the Country whatsoever; that a hundred
Inconveniences, of perhaps greater Moment in themselves, have been
tamely submitted to, with far less Disquietude and Murmurs. And the
Case seemeth yet the harder, if it be true, what many skilful Men assert,
that nothing is more easy than a Remedy; and, that the want of *Silver*,
in Proportion to the little *Gold* remaining among us, is altogether as
unnecessary, as it is inconvenient. A Person of Distinction assured me
very lately, that, in discoursing with the * *Lord Lieutenant*, before his

---

* The Lord *Carteret*.
2 The Pistole and Moidore were, respectively, Spanish and Portuguese gold-coins
frequently used in Ireland and England.

last Return to *England*; his *Excellency* said, *He had pressed the Matter often, in proper Time and Place, and to proper Persons; and could not see any Difficulty of the least Moment, that could prevent us from being made easy upon this Article.*

Whoever carrieth to *England* twenty seven *English* Shillings, and bringeth back one *Moidore*, of full Weight, is a Gainer of Nine-pence *Irish:* In a *Guinea*, the Advantage is Three-pence, and Two-pence in a *Pistole*. The BANKERS, who are generally Masters of all our *Gold* and *Silver*, with this Advantage, have sent over as much of the latter, as came into their Hands. The Value of one thousand *Moidores* in *Silver*, would thus amount in clear Profit to 37 *l*. 10s. The *Shopkeepers*, and other *Traders* who go to *London* to buy Goods, followed the same Practice; by which we have been driven into this insupportable Distress.

To a common Thinker, it should seem that nothing would be more easy, than for the *Government* to redress this Evil, at any Time they shall please. When the Value of *Guineas* was lowered in *England* from 21*s*. and 6*d*. to only 21*s*. the Consequences to this Kingdom were obvious, and manifest to us all: And a sober Man may be allowed at least to wonder, although he dare not complain, why a new Regulation of *Coin* among us, was not then made; much more, why it hath never been since. It would surely require no very profound Skill in *Algebra*, to reduce the Difference of *Nine-pence* in *thirty Shillings*, or *Three-pence* in a *Guinea* to less than a *Farthing*; and so small a Fraction could be no Temptation, either to *Bankers* to hazard their *Silver* at Sea, or Tradesmen to load themselves with it, in their Journies to *England*. In my humble Opinion, it would be no unseasonable Condescension, if the *Government* would graciously please to signify to the *poor loyal Protestant Subjects* of *Ireland*, either that this miserable Want of *Silver*, is not possible to be remedied in any Degree, by the nicest Skill in *Arithmetick*; or else, that it doth not stand with the good Pleasure of *England* to suffer any *Silver* at all among us. In the former Case, it would be Madness to expect Impossibilities; and in the other, we must submit: For, Lives and Fortunes are always at the Mercy of the CONQUEROR.

The Question hath been often put in *printed Papers*, by the DRAPIER and others, or perhaps, by the same WRITER , under different Styles, why this Kingdom should not be permitted to have a *Mint* of its own, for the Coinage of *Gold, Silver*, and *Copper*; which is a Power exercised by many *Bishops*, and every petty prince in *Germany*? But this Question hath never been answered; nor the least Application, that I have heard of, made to the *Crown* from hence, for the Grant of a *Publick Mint*; although it standeth upon

Record, that several Cities and Corporations here, had the Liberty of *Coining Silver*. I can see no Reasons, why we alone of all Nations, are thus restrained; but such as I dare not mention: Only thus far, I may venture; that *Ireland* is the first Imperial Kingdom, since *Nimrod*,[3] which ever wanted Power to *Coin* their own Money.

I know very well, that in *England*, it is lawful for any Subject to petition either the *Prince*, or the *Parliament*, provided it be done in a dutiful and regular Manner: But, what is lawful for a Subject of *Ireland*, I profess I cannot determine: Nor will I undertake, that your *Printer* shall not be prosecuted, in a *Court of Justice*, for publishing my *Wishes*, that a poor Shopkeeper might be able to change a *Guinea*, or a *Moidore*, when a Customer cometh for a *Crown's* Worth of Goods. I have known less Crimes punished with the utmost Severity, under the Title of *Disaffection*. And I cannot but approve the Wisdom of the *Antients*, who, after *Astrea* had fled from the Earth, at least took Care to provide *three upright Judges for Hell*.[4] Mens Ears, among us, are indeed grown so nice, that whoever happeneth to think out of Fashion, in what relateth to the Welfare of this Kingdom, dare not so much as complain of the *Tooth-Ach*; lest our weak and busy Dabblers in Politicks, should be ready to swear against him for *Disaffection*.

There was a Method practised by Sir *Ambrose Crawley*, the great Dealer in *Iron-works*;[5] which I wonder the Gentlemen of our Country, under this great Exigency, have not thought fit to imitate. In the several Towns and Villages where he dealt, and many Miles round; he gave *Notes* instead of *Money*, from *two Pence* to *twenty Shillings*, which passed current in all Shops and Markets, as well as in Houses, where Meat and Drink was sold. I see no Reason, why the like Practice may not be introduced among us, with some Degree of Success. or, at least, may not serve as a poor Expedient, in this our *blessed Age of Paper*; which, as it dischargeth all our greater Payments, may be equally useful in the smaller; and may just keep us alive until an *English Act of Parliament shall forbid it*.

I have been told, that among some of our poorer *American* Colonies upon the Continent, the People enjoy the Liberty of cutting the little Money among them into Halves and Quarters, for the Conveniencies of small Traffick. How happy should we be, in Comparison of our present Condition, if the like Privilege were granted to us, of employing the Sheers, for Want of a *Mint*, upon our *foreign Gold*; by clipping it into *Half-Crowns*, and *Shillings*, and even lower

3 Nimrod, the great hunter, reputed founder of Babylon. Genesis 10:10.
4 Astrea, 'the starry maiden', associated with the constellation Virgo, resided on Earth during the Golden Age, but left during the wickedness of the Bronze Age.
5 I have been unable to trace this figure.

Denominations; for Beggars must be content to live upon Scraps; and it would be our Felicity, that these Scraps could never be exported to other Countries, while any Thing better was left.

If neither of these Projects will avail, I see nothing left us, but to truck and barter our Goods, like the *wild Indians*, with each other; or with our too powerful Neighbours; only with this Disadvantage on our Side, that the *Indians* enjoy the Product of their own Land; whereas the better half of ours is sent away, without so much as a Recompence in *Bugles* or *Glass* in return.[6]

It must needs be a very comfortable Circumstance, in the present Juncture, that some thousand Families are gone, or going, or preparing to go from hence, and settle in *America*. The poorer Sort, for want of Work; the Farmers, whose beneficial Bargains are now become a Rack-Rent too hard to be borne; and those who have any *ready Money*, or can purchase any, by the Sale of their Goods or Leases; because they find their Fortunes hourly decaying, that their Goods will bear no Price, and that few or none have any *Money* to buy the very Necessaries of Life, are hastening to follow their departed Neighbours. It is true, *Corn* among us carrieth a very high Price; but it is for the same Reason, that *Rats*, and *Cats*, and dead *Horses*, have been often bought for *Gold* in a Town besieged.

There is a Person of Quality in my Neighbourhood, who twenty Years ago, when he was just come to Age, being unexperienced, and of a generous Temper, let his Lands, even as Times went then, at a low Rate to able Tenants, and consequently by the Rise of Land since that Time, looked upon his Estate to be set at half Value. But, Numbers of these Tenants, or their Descendants, are now offering to sell their Leases by Cant:[7] even those which were for Lives, some of them renewable for ever, and some Fee-Farms, which the Landlord himself hath bought in at half the Price they would have yielded seven Years ago: And some Leases let at the same Time for Lives, have been given up to him, without any Consideration at all.

This is the most favourable Face of Things at present among us; I say, among us of the *North*, who are esteemed the only thriving People in the Kingdom. And how far, and how soon this Misery and Desolation may spread, is easy to foresee.

The vast Sums of *Money* daily carried off, by our numerous Adventurers to *America*, have deprived us of our *Gold* in these Parts, almost as much as our *Silver*.

And the good Wives who come to our Houses, offer us their Pieces

6 'Bugles' are a kind of ornamental glass-bead.
7 An Irish practice of selling leases by auction to the highest bidder, something Swift deplored.

of Linen, upon which their whole Dependence lies, for so little Profit, that it can neither half pay their Rents, nor half support their Families.

It is remarkable, that this Enthusiasm spread among our *Northern* People, of sheltering themselves in the Continent of *America*, hath no other Foundation, than their present insupportable Condition at Home. I have made all possible Enquiries, to learn what Encouragement our People had met with, by any Intelligence from those Plantations, sufficient to make them undertake so tedious and hazardous a Voyage, in all Seasons of the Year; and so ill accommodated in their Ships, that many of them have died miserably in their Passage; but could never get one satisfactory Answer. Some Body, they knew not who, had written a Letter to his Friend or Cousin from thence, inviting him, by all Means, to come over; that it was a fine fruitful Country, and to be held for ever at a *Penny* an Acre. But the Truth of the Fact is this: The *English* established in those Colonies, are in great Want of Men to inhabit that Tract of Ground, which lieth between them and the *wild Indians*, who are not reduced under their Dominion. We read of some barbarous People, whom the *Romans* placed in their Armies, for no other Service than to blunt their Enemies Swords, and afterwards to fill up Trenches with their dead Bodies. And, thus our People, who transport themseves, are settled in those interjacent Tracts, as a Screen against the Insults of the *Savages*; and may have as much Land as they can clear from the Woods at a very reasonable Rate, if they can afford to pay about a *hundred* Years Purchase, by their Labour. Now, besides the *Fox's* Reasons, which incline all those who have already ventured thither, to represent every Thing in a fair Light, as well for justifying their own Conduct, as for getting Companions in their Misery: The governing People in those Plantations, have also wisely provided, that no Letters shall be suffered to pass from thence hither, without being first viewed by the Council; by which, our People here are wholly deceived, in the Opinions they have of the happy Condition of their Friends gone before them. This was accidentally discovered some Months ago, by an honest Man; who, having transported himself and Family thither, and finding all Things directly contrary to his Hope, had the Luck to convey a private Note, by a faithful Hand, to his Relation here; entreating him not to think of such a Voyage, and to discourage all his Friends from attempting it.

Yet this, although it be a Truth well known, hath produced very little Effect, which is no Manner of Wonder; for, as it is natural for a Man in a *Fever* to turn often, although without any Hope of Ease; or, when he is pursued, to leap down a Precipice, to avoid an

Enemy just at his Back; so Men in the extremest Degree of Misery and Want, will naturally fly to the first Appearance of Relief, let it be ever so vain or visionary.

You may observe, that I have very superficially touched the Subject I began with, and with the utmost Caution: For I know how criminal the least Complaint hath been thought, however reasonable, or just, or honestly intended; which hath forced me to offer up my daily Prayers, that it may never, at least in my Time, be interpreted by *Inuendo's*, as a false, and scandalous, seditious, and disaffected Action, for a Man to roar under an acute Fit of the *Gout*; which, besides the Loss and the Danger, would be very inconvenient to one of my Age, so severely afflicted with that Distemper.

I wish you good Success; but I can promise you little, in an ungrateful Office you have taken up, without the least View, either to Reputation or Profit. Perhaps your Comfort is, that none but *Villains* and *Betrayers* of their Country, can be your *Enemies*. Upon which I have little to say, having not the Honour to be acquainted with many of that Sort; and therefore, as you may easily believe, am compelled to lead a very retired Life.

I am, SIR,
Your most Odedient
Humble Servant,

County of *Down*,
Dec. 2, 1728.   A. NORTH.

AN
ANSWER

TO SEVERAL

LETTERS sent me from unknown Hands.

Written in the year 1729

Written in 1729, this *Answer* was not published until 1765, by Deane Swift in London and Faulkner in Dublin. The essay's pessimism largely explains Swift's decision not to publish. The standardised form of its title reflects his fatigue with being sent so many schemes for consideration and approval. He could never fully resist practical projects for improvement, especially horticultural and agricultural ones, yet he knew that the government would not promote them. *A Modest Proposal*, written in the same year, satirises the absolute lunacy of reforming pamphlets, yet Swift could not stop writing them.

AN

ANSWER

TO SEVERAL

LETTERS sent me from unknown Hands.

Written in the year 1729

I AM very well pleased with the good opinion you express of me, and wish it were any way in my power to answer your expectations, for the service of my country. I have carefully read your several schemes and proposals, which you think should be offered to the parliament. In answer, I will assure you, that, in another place, I have known very good proposals rejected with contempt by public assemblies, merely because they were offered from without doors; and yours perhaps might have the same fate, especially if handed to the publick by me, who am not acquainted with three members, nor have the least interest with one.[1] My printers have been twice prosecuted,[2] to my great expence, on account of discourses I writ for the public service, without the least reflection on parties or persons; and the success I had in those of the Drapier was not owing to my abilities, but to a lucky juncture, when the fuel was ready for the first hand that would be at the pains of kindling it. It is true both those envenomed prosecutions were the workmanship of a judge, who is now gone to his own place*. But, let that be as it will, I am determined henceforth never to be the instrument of leaving an innocent man at the mercy of that bench.

It is certain, there are several particulars relating to this kingdom (I have mentioned a few of them in one of my Drapier's letters), which it were heartily to be wished that the Parliament would take under their consideration, such as will nowise interfere with England, otherwise than to its advantage.

The first I shall mention is touched at in a letter which I received

* Lord Chief-Justice Whitshed.
1 Swift always portrayed himself as a political and social hermit: he may have disliked, but he was not unfamiliar with, many Irish politicians.
2 Edmund Waters for the 1720 *Proposal* and John Harding for the fourth Drapier's letter, *To the Whole People of Ireland*.

from one of you, Gentlemen, about the highways; which, indeed, are almost every where scandalously neglected. I know a very rich man in this city, a true lover and saver of his money, who, being possessed of some adjacent lands, hath been at great charge in repairing effectually the roads that lead to them; and hath assured me, that his lands are thereby advanced four or five shillings an acre, by which he gets treble interest. But, generally speaking, all over the kingdom, the roads are deplorable; and, what is more particularly barbarous, there is no sort of provision made for travellers on foot; no, not near this city, except in a very few places, and in a most wretched manner: whereas the English are so particularly careful in this point, that you may travel there an hundred miles with less inconvenience than one mile here. But, since this may be thought too great a reformation, I shall only speak of roads for horses, carriages, and cattle.

Ireland is, I think, computed to be one third smaller than England; yet, by some natural disadvantages, it would not bear quite the same proportion in value, with the same encouragement. However, it hath so happened, for many years past, that it never arrived to above one eleventh part in point of riches; and, of late, by the continual decrease of trade, and increase of absentees, with other circumstances not here to be mentioned, hardly to a fifteenth part; at least, if my calculations be right, which I doubt are a little too favourable on our side.

Now, supposing day-labour to be cheaper by one half here than in England, and our roads, by the nature of our carriages and the desolation of our country, to be not worn and beaten above one eighth part so much as those of England, which is a very moderate computation; I do not see why the mending of them would be a greater burthen to this kingdom than to that.

There have been, I believe, twenty acts of parliament, in six or seven years of the late king*, for mending long tracts of impassable ways in several counties of England, by erecting turnpikes, and receiving passage-money in a manner that every body knows. If what I have advanced be true, it would be hard to give a reason against the same practice here, since the necessity is as great, the advantage in proportion perhaps much greater, the materials of stone and gravel as easy to be found, and the workmanship at least twice as cheap. Besides, the work may be done gradually, with allowances for the poverty of the nation, by so many perch a year; but with a special care to encourage skill and diligence, and to prevent fraud in the undertakers, to which we are too liable, and which are not always

* King George I.

confined to those of the meaner sort: but against these, no doubt, the wisdom of the nation may, and will provide.

Another evil, which, in my opinion, deserves the public care, is the ill-management of the bogs, the neglect whereof is a much greater mischief to this kingdom than most people seem to be aware of.

It is allowed indeed, by those who are esteemed most skilful in such matters, that the red swelling mossy bog, whereof we have so many large tracts in this island, is not by any means to be fully reduced; but the skirts, which are covered with a green coat, easily may, being not an accretion, or annual growth of moss, like the other.

Now the landlords are generally so careless as to suffer their tenants to cut their turf in these skirts, as well as the bog adjoined, whereby there is yearly lost a considerable quantity of land throughout the kingdom, never to be recovered.

But this is not the greatest part of the mischief. For the main bog, although perhaps not reducible to natural soil, yet, by continuing large, deep, straight canals through the middle, cleaned at proper times, as low as the channel or gravel, would become a secure summer-pasture; the margins might, with great profit and ornament, be filled with quickins,[3] birch, and other trees proper for such a soil, and the canals be convenient for water-carriage of the turf, which is now drawn upon sled-cars with great expence, difficulty, and loss of time, by reason of the many turf-pits scattered irregularly through the bog, wherein great numbers of cattle are yearly drowned. And it hath been, I confess, to me a matter of the greatest vexation as well as wonder, to think how any landlord could be so absurd as to suffer such havock to be made.

All the acts for encouraging plantations of forest-trees are, I am told, extremely defective; which, with great submission, must have been owing to a defect of skill in the contrivers of them. In this climate, by the continual blowing of the West-south-west wind, hardly any tree of value will come to perfection that is not planted in groves, except very rarely, and where there is much land-shelter. I have not, indeed, read all the acts; but, from enquiry, I cannot learn that the planting in groves is enjoined. And, as to the effects of these laws, I have not seen the least, in many hundred miles riding, except about a very few gentlemen's houses, and even those with very little skill or success. In all the rest, the hedges generally miscarry, as well as the larger slender twigs planted upon the tops of ditches, merely for want of common skill and care.

I do not believe that a greater and quicker profit could be made, than by planting large groves of ash, a few feet asunder, which in

3 Mountain-ash or rowan-tree.

seven years would make the best kind of hop-poles,[4] and grow in the same or less time, to a second crop from their roots.

It would likewise be of great use and beauty in our desert scenes, to oblige all tenants and cottagers to plant ash or elm before their cabbins, and round their potatoe-gardens, where cattle either do not, or ought not to come to destroy them.

The common objections against all this, drawn from the laziness, the perverseness, or thievish disposition of the poor native Irish, might be easily answered, by shewing the true reason for such accusations, and how easily those people may be brought to a less savage manner of life: But my printers have already suffered too much for my speculations. However, supposing the size of a native's understanding just equal to that of a dog or horse, I have often seen those two animals to be civilized by rewards, at least as much as by punishments.

It would be a noble atchievement to abolish the Irish language in this kingdom, so far at least as to oblige all the natives to speak only English on every occasion of business, in shops, markets, fairs, and other places of dealing: yet I am wholly deceived if this might not be effectually done in less than half an age, and at a very trifling expence; for such I look upon a tax to be, of only six thousand pounds a year, to accomplish so great a work. This would, in a great measure, civilize the most barbarous among them, reconcile them to our customs and manner of living, and reduce great numbers to the national religion, whatever kind may then happen to be established. The method is plain and simple; and, although I am too desponding to produce it, yet I could heartily wish some public thoughts were employed to reduce this uncultivated people from that idle, savage, beastly, thievish manner of life, in which they continue sunk to a degree, that it is almost impossible for a country gentleman to find a servant of human capacity, or the least tincture of natural honesty; or who does not live among his own tenants in continual fear of having his plantations destroyed, his cattle stolen, and his goods pilfered.

The love, affection, or vanity of living in England, continuing to carry thither so many wealthy families, the consequences thereof, together with the utter loss of all trade, except what is detrimental, which hath forced such great numbers of weavers, and others to seek their bread in foreign countries, the unhappy practice of stocking such vast quantities of land with sheep and other cattle, which reduceth twenty families to one: These events, I say, have exceedingly depopulated this kingdom for several years past. I should heartily

4 Tall poles on which hop-plants are trained for cultivation.

wish, therefore, under this miserable dearth of money, that those who are most concerned would think it adviseable to save a hundred thousand pounds a year, which is now sent out of this kingdom to feed us with corn. There is not an older or more uncontroverted maxim in the politicks of all wise nations, than that of encouraging agriculture.[5] And, therefore, to what kind of wisdom a practice so directly contrary among us may be reduced, I am by no means a judge. If labour and people make the true riches of a nation, what must be the issue where one part of the people are forced away, and the other part have nothing to do?

If it should be thought proper by wiser heads, that his Majesty might be applied to in a national way, for giving the kingdom leave to coin halfpence for its own use; I believe no good subject will be under the least apprehension that such a request could meet with refusal, or the least delay. Perhaps we are the only kingdom upon earth, or that ever was or will be upon earth, which did not enjoy that common right of civil society, under the proper inspection of its prince, or legislature, to coin money of all usual metals for its own occasions.[6] Every petty prince in Germany, vassal to the Emperor, enjoys this privilege. And I have seen in this kingdom several silver pieces, with the inscription of *Civitas Waterford*, *Droghedagh*, and other towns.

---

5 Swift persistently deplored the spread of pasturage and the corresponding decline in tillage, whereby animals replaced people on the land.
6 The same complaint made by the Drapier five years earlier.

MAXIMS

CONTROLLED

IN IRELAND

*The Truth of some Maxims in State and
Government, examined with reference to Ireland.*

Another piece from 1729, but not published until 1765, this essay grew out of notes which Swift had compiled over several years. Using a systematic method of exposition to control his irony, Swift suggests that Ireland's situation defies all current economic theory about the logical or ideal relation between population, natural resources and prosperity. In this sense, Ireland 'controls', or 'contradicts', most received wisdom about a healthy economy. In his view, absentee-landlords are the primary culprits of this unnatural state of affairs. Without the political liberty enjoyed by most European nations, he argues, all plans for Irish economic improvement are a wasted effort.

MAXIMS

CONTROLLED

IN IRELAND

*The Truth of some Maxims in State and Government,
examined with reference to Ireland.*

THERE are certain Maxims of State, founded upon long observations and experience, drawn from the constant practice of the wisest nations, and from the very principles of government, nor ever controlled by any writer upon politics. Yet all these maxims do necessarily pre-suppose a kingdom, or commonwealth, to have the same natural rights common to the rest of mankind who have entered into civil society. For, if we could conceive a nation where each of the inhabitants had but one eye, one leg, and one hand, it is plain that, before you could institute them into a republic, an allowance must be made for those material defects, wherein they differed from other mortals. Or, imagine a legislator forming a system for the government of Bedlam, and, proceeding upon the maxim that man is a sociable animal, should draw them out of their cells, and form them into corporations, or general assemblies; the consequence might probably be, that they would fall foul on each other, or burn the house over their own heads.

Of the like nature are innumerable errors, committed by crude and short thinkers, who reason upon general topics, without the least allowance for the most important circumstances, which quite alter the nature of the case.

This hath been the fate of those small dealers, who are every day publishing their thoughts either on paper or in their assemblies for improving the trade of Ireland, and referring us to the practice and example of England, Holland, France, or other nations.

I shall therefore examine certain Maxims of government, which generally pass for uncontrolled in the world, and consider how far they will suit with the present condition of this kingdom.

First, it is affirmed by wise men, that the dearness of things necessary for life, in a fruitful country, is a certain sign of wealth and great commerce: For, when such necessaries are dear, it must absolutely follow, that money is cheap and plentiful.

But this is manifestly false in Ireland, for the following reason.

Some years ago, the species of money here, did probably amount to six or seven hundred thousand pounds; and I have good cause to believe, that our remittances then did not much exceed the cash brought in to us. But the prodigious discouragements we have since received in every branch of our trade, by the frequent enforcements, and rigorous execution of the navigation-act,[1] the tyranny of under custom-house officers, the yearly addition of absentees, the payments to regiments abroad, to civil and military officers residing in England, the unexpected sudden demands of great sums from the treasury, and some other drains of, perhaps, as great consequence, we now see ourselves reduced to a state (since we have no friends) of being pitied by our enemies, at least, if our enemies were of such a kind as to be capable of any regards towards us, except of hatred and contempt.

Forty years are now passed since the Revolution, when the contention of the British empire was, most unfortunately for us, and altogether against the usual course of such mighty changes in government, decided in the least important nation, but with such ravages and ruin executed on both sides, as to leave the kingdom a desert, which, in some sort, it still continues. Neither did the long rebellions in 1641, make half such a destruction of houses, plantations, and personal wealth, in both kingdoms, as two years campaigns did in ours, by fighting England's battles.[2]

By slow degrees, and by the gentle treatment we received under two auspicious reigns, we grew able to live without running in debt. Our absentees were but few, we had great indulgence in trade, a considerable share in employments of church and state; and, while the short leases continued, which were let some years after the war ended, tenants paid their rents with ease and chearfulness, to the great regret of their landlords, who had taken up a spirit of oppression that is not easily removed. And although, in these short leases, the rent was gradually to encrease after short periods; yet, as soon as the term elapsed, the land was let to the highest bidder, most commonly without the least effectual clause for building or planting. Yet, by many advantages which this island then possessed, and hath since utterly lost, the rents of lands still grew higher upon every lease that expired, until they have arrived at the present exorbitance; when the frog, overswelling himself, burst at last.

1 The Navigation Act of 1663, the first of several pieces of legislation passed during Charles II's reign, which prohibited the exportation of Irish goods seen to be competing with England's foreign trade.
2 A bitter irony for Swift, who often pointed to the fact that the British constitution was achieved at the expense of Irish Protestants, and on Irish soil.

With the price of land, of necessity rose that of corn and cattle, and all other commodities that farmers deal in: Hence likewise, obviously, the rates of all goods and manufactures among shop-keepers, the wages of servants, and hire of labourers. But, although our miseries came on fast, with neither trade nor money left, yet neither will the landlord abate in his rent, nor can the tenant abate in the price of what that rent must be paid with, nor any shopkeeper, tradesman, or labourer live, at lower expence, for food and cloathing, than he did before.

I have been the larger upon this first head, because the same obser-vations will clear up and strengthen a good deal of what I shall affirm upon the rest.

The second Maxim of those who reason upon trade and govern-ment, is to assert, that low interest is a certain sign of great plenty of money in a nation, for which, as in many other articles, they pro-duce the examples of Holland and England. But, with relation to Ireland, this Maxim is likewise entirely false.

There are two reasons for the lowness of interest in any country. First, that which is usually alledged, the great plenty of species; and this is obvious. The second is the want of trade, which seldom falls under common observation, although it be equally true. For, where trade is altogether discouraged, there are few borrowers. In those countries where men can employ a large stock, the young merchant, whose fortune may be four or five hundred pounds, will venture to borrow as much more, and can afford a reasonable interest. Neither is it easy at this day to find many of those, whose business reaches to employ even so inconsiderable a sum, except among the importers of wine; who, as they have most part of the present trade in these parts of Ireland in their hands, so they are the most exorbi-tant, exacting, fraudulent dealers, that ever trafficked in any nation, and are making all possible speed to ruin both themselves and the nation.

From this defect, of gentlemen's not knowing how to dispose of their ready money, ariseth the high purchase of lands, which in all other countries is reckoned a sign of wealth. For, the frugal squires, who live below their incomes, have no other way to dispose of their savings but by mortgage or purchase, by which the rates of land must naturally encrease; and, if this trade continues long under the uncertainty of rents, the landed men of ready money will find it more for their advantage to send their cash to England, and place it in the funds; which I myself am determined to do, the first considerable sum I shall be master of.

It hath likewise been a Maxim among politicians, that the great encrease of buildings in the metropolis, argues a flourishing state. But this, I confess, hath been controlled from the example of London; where, by the long and annual parliamentary sessions, such a number of senators, with their families, friends, adherents, and expectants, draw such prodigious numbers to that city, that the old hospitable custom of lords and gentlemen living in their antient seats, among their tenants, is almost lost in England; is laughed out of doors; insomuch that, in the middle of summer, a legal House of Lords and Commons might be brought in a few hours to London, from their country villas within twelve miles round.

The case in Ireland is yet somewhat worse: For the absentees of great estates, who, if they lived at home, would have many rich retainers in their neighbourhoods, having learned to rack their lands, and shorten their leases, as much as any residing squire; and the few remaining of these latter, having some vain hope of employments for themselves or their children, and discouraged by the beggarliness and thievery of their own miserable farmers and cottagers, or seduced by the vanity of their wives, on pretence of their children's education, (whereof the fruits are so apparent) together with that most wonderful, and yet more unaccountable zeal, for a seat in their assembly, though at some years purchase of their whole estates. These, and some other motives, better let pass, have drawn such a concourse to this beggarly city, that the dealers of the several branches of building, have found out all the commodious and inviting places for erecting new houses, while fifteen hundred of the old ones, which is a seventh part of the whole city, are said to be left uninhabited, and falling to ruin. Their method is the same with that which was first introduced by Doctor Barebone at London, who died a bankrupt.[3] The mason, the bricklayer, the carpenter, the slater, and the glazier, take a lot of ground, club to build one or more houses, unite their credit, their stock, and their money, and when their work is finished, sell it to the best advantage they can. But, as it often happens, and more every day, that their fund will not answer half their design, they are forced to undersel it at the first story, and are all reduced to beggary. Insomuch, that I know a certain fanatic brewer*, who is reported to have some hundreds of houses in this town, is said

---

* Leeson [The Leeson family came to Ireland around 1680, and quickly became wealthy through their brewing and land-speculation businesses. Joseph Leeson was the best-known for his enterprise in developing old parts of Dublin into new sites. One of the main streets of Georgian Dublin is named after him]

3 Nicholas Barbon (d.1698). After the great fire of 1666, one of the major building speculators in London, during which work he invented the idea of fire-insurance. Author of several treatises on money and trade. Died owing millions of pounds to creditors.

to have purchased the greater part of them at half value, from ruined undertakers, hath intelligence of all new houses where the finishing is at a stand, takes advantage of the builder's distress, and, by the advantage of ready money, gets fifty *per cent.* at least for his bargain.

It is another undisputed maxim in government, that people are the riches of the nation; which is so universally granted, that it will be hardly pardonable to bring it in doubt.[4] And I will grant it to be so far true, even in this island, that, if we had the African custom or privilege, of selling our useless bodies for slaves to foreigners, it would be the most useful branch of our trade, by ridding us of a most insupportable burthen, and bringing us money in the stead. But, in our present situation, at least five children in six who are born, lie a dead weight upon us for want of employment. And a very skilful computer assured me, that above one half of the souls in this kingdom supported themselves by begging and thievery, whereof two thirds would be able to get their bread in any other country upon earth. Trade is the only incitement to labour: where that fails, the poorer native must either beg, steal, or starve, or be forced to quit his country. This hath made me often wish, for some years past, that, instead of discouraging our people from seeking foreign soil, that the public would rather pay for transporting all our unnecessary mortals, whether Papists, or Protestants, to America, as drawbacks are sometimes allowed for exporting commodities, where a nation is over-stocked. I confess myself to be touched with a very sensible pleasure, when I hear of a mortality in any country parish or village, where the wretches are forced to pay for a filthy cabin and two ridges of potatoes treble the worth, brought up to steal or beg, for want of work, to whom death would be the best thing to be wished for, on account both of themselves and the public.

Among all taxes imposed by the legislature, those upon luxury are universally allowed to be the most equitable and beneficial to the subject; and the commonest reasoner on government might fill a volume with arguments on the subject. Yet here again, by the singular fate of Ireland, this maxim is utterly false; and the putting it in practice may have such a pernicious consequence, as I certainly believe the thoughts of the proposers were not able to reach.

The miseries we suffer by our absentees, are of a far more

---

4 Current mercantilist wisdom about economic value of a large population. A maxim 'controlled' with devastating irony in *A Modest Proposal*, written shortly after this essay. The entire paragraph here contains many of the ideas and images which make up the outrageous arguments of the subsequent pamphlet.

extensive nature than seems to be commonly understood. I must vindicate myself to the reader so far, as to declare solemnly, that what I shall say of those lords and squires, doth not arise from the least regard I have for their understandings, their virtues, or their persons. For, although I have not the honour of the least acquaintance with any one among them, (my ambition not soaring so high) yet I am too good a witness of the situation they have been in for thirty years past, the veneration paid them by the people, the high esteem they are in among the prime nobility and gentry, the particular marks of favour and distinction they receive from the court: The weight and consequence of their interest, added to their great zeal and application for preventing any hardships their country might suffer from England, wisely considering that their own fortunes and honours were embarked in the same bottom.

A MODEST
PROPOSAL

FOR

Preventing the Children of poor People in Ireland, from being a Burden to their Parents or Country; and for making them beneficial to the Publick.

Written in the Year 1729

A Modest Proposal is undoubtedly Swift's best-known pamphlet, but often read without an appreciation of its place in Swift's Irish career: its ironies are historical as well as rhetorical. It first appeared, anonymously, in October 1729, and was reprinted several times in Dublin and London over the following years, including Pope's *Miscellanies: The Third Volume* (1732).

A MODEST
PROPOSAL
FOR

Preventing the Children of poor People in Ireland, *from being a Burden to their Parents or Country; and for making them beneficial to the Publick.*

Written in the Year 1729

IT is a mellancholly Object to those, who walk through this great Town, or travel in the Country; when they see the *Streets*, the *Roads*, and *Cabbins-doors* crowded with *Beggars* of the Female Sex, followed by three, four, or six Children, *all in Rags*, and importuning every Passenger for an Alms. These *Mothers*, instead of being able to work for their honest Livelyhood, are forced to employ all their Time in stroling to beg Sustenance for their *helpless Infants*; who, as they grow up, either turn *Thieves* for want of Work; or leave their *dear Native Country, to fight for the Pretender in* Spain;[1] or sell themselves to the *Barbadoes.*

I think it is agreed by all Parties, that this prodigious Number of Children in the Arms, or on the Backs, or at the *Heels* of their *Mothers,* and frequently of their *Fathers, is in the present deplorable State of the Kingdom,* a very great additional Grievance; and therefore, whoever could find out a fair, cheap, and easy Method of making these Children sound and useful Members of the Commonwealth; would deserve so well of the Publick, as to have his Statue set up for a Preserver of the Nation.

But my Intention is very far from being confined to provide only for the Children of *professed Beggars*: It is of a much greater Extent, and shall take in the whole Number of Infants at a certain Age, who are born of Parents, in effect as little able to support them, as those who demand our Charity in the Streets.

As to my own Part, having turned my Thoughts for many Years,

---

1 From political allusions like this, Swift's projector makes it clear that he is talking about the Catholic peasantry. Albeit in an ironic form, this is the first time such a class is considered with any sympathy.

upon this important Subject; and maturely weighed the several *Schemes of other Projectors*, I have always found them grosly mistaken in their Computation. It is true, a Child *just dropt from its Dam*, may be supported by her Milk, for a Solar Year with little other Nourishment; at most not above the Value of two Shillings; which the Mother may certainly get, or the Value in *Scraps*, by her lawful Occupation of *Begging*: And, it is exactly at one Year old, that I propose to provide for them in such a Manner, as, instead of being a Charge upon their *Parents*, or the *Parish*, or *wanting Food and Raiment* for the rest of their Lives; they shall, on the contrary, contribute to the Feeding, and partly to the Cloathing, of many Thousands.

There is likewise another great Advantage in my *Scheme*, that it will prevent those *voluntary Abortions*, and that horrid Practice of *Women murdering their Bastard Children*; alas! too frequent among us; sacrificing the *poor innocent Babes*, I doubt, more to avoid the Expence than the Shame; which would move Tears and Pity in the most Savage and inhuman Breast.

The Number of Souls in *Ireland* being usually reckoned one Million and a half,[2] of these I calculate there may be about Two Hundred Thousand Couple whose Wives are Breeders; from which Number I substract thirty thousand Couples, who are able to maintain their own Children; although I apprehend there cannot be so many, under *the present Distresses of the Kingdom*; but this being granted, there will remain an Hundred and Seventy Thousand Breeders. I again substract Fifty Thousand, for those Women who miscarry, or whose Children die by Accident, or Disease, within the Year. There only remain an Hundred and Twenty Thousand Children of poor Parents, annually born: The Question therefore is, How this Number shall be reared, and provided for? Which, as I have already said, under the present Situation of Affairs, is utterly impossible, by all the Methods hitherto proposed: For we can *neither employ them in Handicraft* or *Agriculture*; we neither build Houses, (I mean in the Country) nor cultivate Land: They can very seldom pick up a Livelyhood *by Stealing* until they arrive at six Years old; except where they are of towardly Parts; although, I confess, they learn the Rudiments much earlier; during which Time, they can, however, be properly looked upon only as *Probationers*; as I have been informed by a principal Gentleman in the County of *Cavan*,[3] who protested to

---

2 Most likely an underestimation or guesswork. There is no scholarly consensus on Ireland's population at this time, but it is generally reckoned to be closer to three or four millions.

3 Thomas Sheridan? Swift was quite familiar with Cavan, where he regularly visited Sheridan, and with the bordering county of Armagh, where he passed the summer of 1729 with the Achesons of Markethill.

me, that he never knew above one or two Instances under the Age of six, even in a Part of the Kingdom *so renowned for the quickest Proficiency in that Art.*

I am assured by our Merchants, that a Boy or a Girl before twelve Years old, is no saleable Commodity; and even when they come to this Age, they will not yield above Three Pounds, or Three Pounds and half a Crown at most, on the Exchange; which cannot turn to Account either to the Parents or Kingdom; the Charge of Nutriment and Rags, having been at least four Times that Value.

I shall now therefore humbly propose my own Thoughts; which I hope will not be liable to the least Objection.

I have been assured by a very knowing *American* of my Acquaintance in *London;*[4] that a young healthy Child, well nursed, is, at a Year old, a most delicious, nourishing, and wholesome Food; whether *Stewed, Roasted, Baked,* or *Boiled*; and, I make no doubt, that it will equally serve in a *Fricasie,* or *Ragoust.*

I do therefore humbly offer it to *publick Consideration,* that of the Hundred and Twenty thousand Children, already computed, Twenty thousand may be reserved for Breed; whereof only one Fourth Part to be Males; which is more than we allow to *Sheep, black Cattle,* or *Swine*; and my Reason is, that these Children are seldom the Fruits of Marriage, a *Circumstance not much regarded by our Savages*; therefore, *one Male* will be sufficient to serve *four Females.* That the remaining Hundred thousand, may, at a Year old, be offered in Sale to the *Persons of Quality* and *Fortune,* through the Kingdom; always advising the Mother to let them suck plentifully in the last Month, so as to render them plump, and fat for a good Table. A Child will make two Dishes at an Entertainment for Friends; and when the Family dines alone, the fore or hind Quarter will make a reasonable Dish; and seasoned with a little Pepper or Salt, will be very good Boiled on the fourth Day, especially in *Winter.*

I have reckoned upon a Medium,[5] that a Child just born will weigh Twelve Pounds; and in a solar Year, if tolerably nursed, encreaseth to twenty eight Pounds.

I grant this Food will be somewhat dear, and therefore very *proper for Landlords*; who, as they have already devoured most of the Parents, seem to have the best Title to the Children.

Infants Flesh will be in Season throughout the Year; but more

---

4 The point of the American informant is to highlight an authority familiar with settlement amongst barbarous natives. Many emigrants from Ireland, especially Ulster Presbyterians, had sent back reports from America on their fortunes in the new colony.

5 On average.

plentiful in *March*, and a little before and after: For we are told by
a grave * Author, an eminent *French* Physician, that *Fish being a
prolifick Dyet*, there are more Children born in *Roman Catholick
Countries* about Nine Months after *Lent*, than at any other Season:
Therefore reckoning a Year after *Lent*, the markets will be more glut-
ted than usual; because the Number of *Popish Infants*, is, at least,
three to one in this Kingdom; and therefore it will have one other
Collateral Advantage, by lessening the Number of *Papists* among us.

I have already computed the Charge of nursing a Beggar's Child
(in which List I reckon all *Cottagers*, *Labourers*, and Four fifths of
the *Farmers*) to be about two Shillings *per Annum*, Rags included;
and I believe, no Gentleman would repine to give Ten Shillings for
the *Carcase of a good fat Child*; which, as I have said, will make
four Dishes of excellent nutritive Meat, when he hath only some particular Friend, or his own Family, to dine with him. Thus the Squire
will learn to be a good Landlord, and grow popular among his
Tenants; the Mother will have Eight Shillings net Profit, and be fit
for Work until she produceth another Child.

Those who are more thrifty (*as I must confess the Times require*)
may flay the Carcase; the Skin of which, artificially dressed, will
make admirable *Gloves for Ladies*, and *Summer Boots for fine
Gentlemen*.

As to our City of *Dublin*; Shambles may be appointed for this
Purpose, in the most convenient Parts of it; and Butchers we may
be assured will not be wanting; although I rather recommend buying the Children alive, and dressing them hot from the Knife, as we
do *roasting Pigs*.

A very worthy Person, *a true Lover of his Country*, and whose
Virtues I highly esteem, was lately pleased, in discoursing on this
Matter, to offer a Refinement upon my Scheme. He said, that many
Gentlemen of this Kingdom, having of late destroyed their Deer; he
conceived, that the Want of Venison might be well supplied by the
Bodies of young Lads and Maidens, not exceeding fourteen Years
of Age, nor under twelve; so great a Number of both Sexes in every
County being now ready to starve, for Want of Work and Service:
And these to be disposed of by their Parents, if alive, or otherwise
by their nearest Relations. But with due Deference to so excellent
a Friend, and so deserving a Patriot, I cannot be altogether in his
Sentiments. For as to the Males, my *American* Acquaintance assured
me from frequent Experience, that their Flesh was generally tough
and lean, like that of our School-boys, by continual Exercise; and
their Taste disagreeable; and to fatten them would not answer the

* Rabelais.

Charge. Then, as to the Females, it would, I think, with humble Submission, *be a Loss to the Publick*, because they soon would become Breeders themselves: And besides it is not improbable, that some scrupulous People might be apt to censure such a Practice (although indeed very unjustly) as a little bordering upon Cruelty; which, I confess, hath always been with me the strongest Objection against any Project, how well soever intended.

But in order to justify my Friend: he confessed, that this Expedient was put into his Head by the famous *Salmanaazor*,[6] a Native of the Island *Formosa*, who came from thence to *London*, above twenty Years ago, and in Conversation told my Friend, that in his Country, when any young Person happened to be put to Death, the Executioner sold the Carcase to *Persons of Quality*, as a prime Dainty; and that, in his Time, the Body of a plump Girl of fifteen, who was crucified for an Attempt to poison the Emperor, was sold to his Imperial *Majesty's prime Minister of State*, and other great *Mandarines* of the Court, *in Joints from the Gibbet*, at Four hundred Crowns. Neither indeed can I deny, that if the same Use were made of several plump young Girls in this Town, who, without one single Groat to their Fortunes, cannot stir Abroad without a Chair, and appear at a *Play house*, and *Assemblies* in foreign Fineries, which they never will pay for; the Kingdom would not be the worse.

Some Persons of a desponding Spirit are in great Concern about that vast Number of poor People, who are Aged, Diseased, or Maimed; and I have been desired to employ my Thoughts what Course may be taken, to ease the Nation of so grievous an Incumbrance. But I am not in the least Pain upon that Matter; because it is very well known, that they are every Day *dying*, and *rotting*, by *Cold* and *Famine*, and *Filth*, and *Vermin*, as fast as can be reasonably expected. And as to the younger Labourers, they are now in almost as hopeful a Condition: They cannot get Work, and consequently pine away for Want of Nourishment, to a Degree, that if at any Time they are accidentally hired to common Labour, they have not Strength to perform it; and thus the Country, and themselves, are in a fair Way of being soon delivered from the Evils to come.

I have too long digressed; and therefore shall return to my Subject. I think the Advantages by the Proposal which I have made, are obvious, and many, as well as of the highest Importance.

For, *First*, as I have already observed, it would greatly lessen *the Number of Papists*, with whom we are yearly over run; being the principal Breeders of the Nation, as well as our most dangerous

6 George Psalmanazar, French literary impostor, had published a well-known fictional history of Formosa in 1704.

Enemies; and who stay at home on Purpose, with a Design *to deliver the Kingdom to the Pretender*; hoping to take their Advantage by the Absence *of so many good Protestants*, who have chosen rather to leave their Country, than stay at home, and pay Tithes against their Conscience, to an idolatrous *Episcopal Curate*.

Secondly, The poorer Tenants will have something valuable of their own, which, by Law, may be made liable to Distress, and help to pay their Landlord's Rent; their Corn and Cattle being already seized, and *Money a Thing unknown*.

Thirdly, Whereas the Maintenance of an Hundred Thousand Children, from two Years old, and upwards, cannot be computed at less then ten Shillings a Piece *per Annum*, the Nation's Stock will be thereby encreased Fifty Thousand Pounds *per Annum*; besides the Profit of a new Dish, introduced to the Tables of all *Gentlemen of Fortune* in the Kingdom, who have any Refinement in Taste; and the Money will circulate among our selves, the Goods being entirely of our own Growth and Manufacture.[7]

Fourthly, The constant Breeders, besides the Gain of Eight Shillings *Sterling per Annum*, by the Sale of their Children, will be rid of the Charge of maintaining them after the first Year.

Fifthly, This Food would likewise bring great *Custom to Taverns*, where the Vintners will certainly be so prudent, as to procure the best Receipts for dressing it to Perfection; and consequently, have their Houses frequented by all the *fine Gentlemen*, who justly value themselves upon their Knowledge in good Eating; and a skilful Cook, who understands how to oblige his Guests, will contrive to make it as expensive as they please.

Sixthly, This would be a great Inducement to Marriage, which all wise Nations have either encouraged by Rewards, or enforced by Laws and Penalties. It would encrease the Care and Tenderness of Mothers towards their Children, when they were sure of a Settlement for Life, to the poor Babes, provided in some Sort by the Publick, to their annual Profit instead of Expence. We should soon see an honest Emulation among the married Women, *which of them could bring the fattest Child to the Market*. Men would become as *fond* of their Wives, during the Time of their Pregnancy, as they are now of their *Mares* in Foal, their *Cows* in Calf, or *Sows* when they are ready to farrow; nor offer to beat or kick them, (as it is too *frequent a* Practice) for fear of a Miscarriage.

Many other Advantages might be enumerated. For Instance, the Addition of some Thousand Carcasses in our Exportation of barrelled Beef: The Propagation of *Swines Flesh*, and Improvement in the

7 A triumphant irony, confirming the good sense of Swift's 1720 *Proposal*.

Art of making good *Bacon*; so much wanted among us by the great Destruction of *Pigs*, too frequent at our Tables, and are no way comparable in Taste, or Magnificence, to a well-grown fat yearly Child; which, roasted whole, will make a considerable Figure at a *Lord Mayor's Feast*, or any other publick Entertainment. But this, and many others, I omit; being studious of Brevity.

Supposing that one Thousand Families in this City, would be constant Customers for Infants Flesh; besides others who might have it at *merry Meetings*, particularly at *Weddings* and *Christenings*; I compute that *Dublin* would take off, annually, about Twenty Thousand Carcasses; and the rest of the Kingdom (where probably they will be sold somewhat cheaper) the remaining Eighty Thousand.

I can think of no one Objection, that will possibly be raised against this Proposal; unless it should be urged, that the Number of People will be thereby much lessened in the Kingdom. This I freely own; and it was indeed one principal Design in offering it to the World. I desire the Reader will observe, that I calculate my Remedy *for this one individual Kingdom of* IRELAND, *and for no other that ever was, is, or I think ever can be upon Earth.* Therefore, let no Man talk to me of other Expedients:[8] *Of taxing our Absentees at five Shillings a Pound: Of using neither Cloaths, nor Houshold Furniture; except what is of our own Growth and Manufacture: Of utterly rejecting the Materials and Instruments that promote foreign Luxury: Of curing the Expensiveness of Pride, Vanity, Idleness, and Gaming in our Women: Of introducing a Vein of Parsimony, Prudence and Temperance: Of learning to love our Country; wherein we differ even from* LAPLANDERS, *and the Inhabitants of* TOPINAMBOO:[9] *Of quitting our Animosities, and Factions; nor act any longer like the* Jews, *who were murdering one another at the very Moment their City was taken: Of being a little cautious not to sell our Country and Consciences for nothing: Of teaching Landlords to have, at least, one Degree of Mercy towards their Tenants. Lastly, Of putting a Spirit of Honesty, Industry, and Skill into our Shop-keepers; who, if a Resolution could now be taken to buy only our native Goods, would immediately unite to cheat and exact upon us in the Price, the Measure, and the Goodness; nor could ever yet be brought to make one fair Proposal of just Dealing, though often and earnestly invited to it.*

Therefore I repeat; let no Man talk to me of these and the like Expedients; till he hath, at least, a Glimpse of Hope, that there will

8 What follows, of course, is a catalogue of Swift's earlier and unambiguous proposals. An irony best appreciated by those familiar with them.
9 Primitive region of Brazil.

ever be some hearty and sincere Attempt to put *them in Practice.*

But, as to my self; having been wearied out for many Years with offering vain, idle, visionary Thoughts; and at length utterly despairing of Success, I fortunately fell upon this Proposal; which, as it is wholly new, so it hath something *solid* and *real*, of no Expence, and little Trouble, full in our own Power; and whereby we can incur no Danger in *disobliging* ENGLAND: For, this Kind of Commodity will not bear Exportation; the Flesh being of too tender a Consistence, to admit a long Continuance in Salt; *although, perhaps, I could name a Country, which would be glad to eat up our whole Nation without it.*

After all, I am not so violently bent upon my own Opinion, as to reject any Offer proposed by wise Men, which shall be found equally innocent, cheap, easy, and effectual. But before something of that Kind shall be advanced, in Contradiction to my Scheme, and offering a better; I desire the Author, or Authors, will be pleased maturely to consider two Points. *First,* As Things now stand, how they will be able to find Food and Raiment, for a Hundred Thousand useless Mouths and Backs? And *secondly,* There being a round Million of Creatures in human Figure, throughout this Kingdom; whose whole Subsistence, put into a common Stock, would leave them in Debt two Millions of Pounds *Sterling*; adding those, who are Beggars by Profession, to the Bulk of Farmers, Cottagers, and Labourers, with their Wives and Children, who are Beggars in Effect; I desire those Politicians, who dislike my Overture, and may perhaps be so bold to attempt an Answer, that they will first ask the Parents of these Mortals, Whether they would not, at this Day, think it a great Happiness to have been sold for Food at a Year old, in the Manner I prescribe; and thereby have avoided such a perpetual Scene of Misfortunes, as they have since gone through; by the *Oppression of Landlords*; the Impossibility of paying Rent, without Money or Trade; the Want of common Sustenance, with neither House nor Cloaths, to cover them from the Inclemencies of Weather; and the most inevitable Prospect of intailing the like, or greater Miseries upon their Breed for ever.

I profess, in the Sincerity of my Heart, that I have not the least personal Interest, in endeavouring to promote this necessary Work; having no other Motive than the *publick Good of my Country, by advancing our Trade, providing for Infants, relieving the Poor, and giving some Pleasure to the Rich.* I have no Children, by which I can propose to get a single Penny; the youngest being nine Years old, and my Wife past Child-bearing.

SERMON
CAUSES
OF THE
WRETCHED CONDITION
OF
IRELAND.

We should never forget that Swift's pamphleteering spirit owes much to his pastoral role. One of the eleven surviving sermons preached by him, *Causes of the Wretched Condition of Ireland* shows the inseparability, for Swift, of religious and civic responsibilities. It also shows him at his most puritanical on the problem of poverty. He took his duty as a preacher very seriously, but never regarded his sermons as part of his literary career. After his death, however, the surviving texts of his sermons were published in Dublin and London. The present sermon was first published, along with two others, in 1762 by Faulkner. We do not know the exact date of its original composition, but it was probably in the early 1730s. See Louis Landa's *Introduction to the Sermons, Prose Works* IX, pp. 95–137.

SERMON

CAUSES

OF THE

WRETCHED CONDITION

OF

IRELAND.

Psalm CXLIV. Part of the 13th and 14th Ver.

That there be no Complaining in our Streets.
Happy is the People that is in such a Case.

IT is a very melancholy Reflection, that such a Country as ours, which is capable of producing all Things necessary, and most Things convenient for Life, sufficient for the Support of four Times the Number of its Inhabitants, should yet lye under the heaviest Load of Misery and Want, our Streets crouded with Beggars, so many of our lower Sort of Tradesmen, Labourers and Artificers, not able to find Cloaths and Food for their Families.[1]

I think it may therefore be of some Use, to lay before you the chief Causes of this wretched Condition we are in, and then it will be easier to assign what Remedies are in our Power towards removing, at least, some Part of these Evils.

For it is ever to be lamented, that we lie under many Disadvantages, not by our own Faults, which are peculiar to ourselves, and which no other Nation under Heaven hath any Reason to complain of.

I shall, therefore first mention some Causes of our Miseries, which I doubt are not to be remedied, until God shall put it in the Hearts

---

1 An opening remarkably similar to that of *A Modest Proposal*, suggesting a date very close to 1729.

of those who are the stronger, to allow us the common Rights and Privileges of Brethren, Fellow-Subjects, and even of Mankind.

The first Cause of our Misery is the intolerable Hardships we lie under in every Branch of our Trade, by which we are become as *Hewers of Wood, and Drawers of Water*, to our rigorous Neighbours.

The second Cause of our miserable State is the Folly, the Vanity, and Ingratitude of those vast Numbers, who think themselves too good to live in the Country which gave them Birth, and still gives them Bread; and rather chuse to pass their Days, and consume their Wealth, and draw out the very Vitals of their Mother Kingdom, among those who heartily despise them.

These I have but lightly touched on, because I fear they are not to be redressed, and, besides, I am very sensible how ready some People are to take Offence at the honest Truth; and, for that Reason, I shall omit several other Grievances, under which we are long likely to groan.

I shall therefore go on to relate some other Causes of this Nation's Poverty, by which, if they continue much longer, it must infallibly sink to utter Ruin.

The first is, that monstrous Pride and Vanity in both Sexes, especially the weaker Sex, who, in the Midst of Poverty, are suffered to run into all Kind of Expence and Extravagance in Dress, and particularly priding themselves to wear nothing but what cometh from Abroad, disdaining the Growth or Manufacture of their own Country, in those Articles where they can be better served at Home with half the Expence; and this is grown to such a Height, that they will carry the whole yearly Rent of a good Estate at once on their Body. And, as there is in that Sex a Spirit of Envy, by which they cannot endure to see others in a better Habit than themselves; so those, whose Fortunes can hardly support their Families in the Necessaries of Life, will needs vye with the Richest and Greatest amongst us, to the Ruin of themselves and their Posterity.

Neither are the Men less guilty of this pernicious Folly, who, in Imitation of a Gaudiness and Foppery of Dress, introduced of late Years into our neighbouring Kingdom, (as Fools are apt to imitate only the Defects of their Betters) cannot find Materials in their own Country worthy to adorn their Bodies of Clay, while their Minds are naked of every valuable Quality.

Thus our Tradesmen and Shopkeepers, who deal in Home-Goods, are left in a starving Condition, and only those encouraged who ruin the Kingdom by importing among us foreign Vanities.

Another Cause of our low Condition is our great Luxury, the chief

Support of which is the Materials of it brought to the Nation in Exchange for the few valuable Things left us, whereby so many thousand Families want the very Necessaries of Life.

Thirdly, in most Parts of this Kingdom the Natives are from their Infancy so given up to Idleness and Sloth, that they often chuse to beg or steal, rather than support themselves with their own Labour; they marry without the least View or Thought of being able to make any Provision for their Families; and whereas, in all industrious Nations, Children are looked on as a Help to their Parents, with us, for want of being early trained to work, they are an intolerable Burthen at Home, and a grievous Charge upon the Public, as appeareth from the vast Number of ragged and naked Children in Town and Country, led about by stroling Women, trained up in Ignorance and all Manner of Vice.

Lastly, A great Cause of this Nation's Misery, is that *Ægyptian* Bondage of cruel, oppressing, covetous Landlords, expecting that all who live under them should *make Bricks without Straw*, who grieve and envy when they see a Tenant of their own in a whole Coat, or able to afford one comfortable Meal in a Month, by which the Spirits of the People are broken, and made for Slavery; the Farmers and Cottagers, almost through the whole Kingdom, being to all Intents and Purposes as real Beggars, as any of those to whom we give our Charity in the Streets. And these cruel Landlords are every Day unpeopling their Kingdom, by forbidding their miserable Tenants to till the Earth, against common Reason and Justice, and contrary to the practice and Prudence of all other Nations, by which numberless Families have been forced either to leave the Kingdom, or stroll about, and increase the Number of our Thieves and Beggars.

Such, and much worse, is our Condition at present, if I had Leisure or Liberty to lay it before you; and, therefore, the next Thing which might be considered is, whether there may be any probable Remedy found, at the least against some Part of these Evils; for most of them are wholly desperate.

But this being too large a Subject to be now handled, and the Intent of my Discourse confining me to give some Directions concerning the Poor of this City, I shall keep myself within those Limits. It is indeed in the Power of the Lawgivers to found a School in every Parish of the Kingdom, for teaching the meaner and poorer Sort of Children to speak and read the English Tongue, and to provide a reasonable Maintenance for the Teachers.[2] This would, in Time,

2 Swift had little or no knowledge of the language of the Gaelic-speaking majority: like so many colonists, he regularly urged schemes to abolish Gaelic in the interests of civilisation.

abolish that Part of Barbarity and Ignorance, for which our Natives
are so despised by all Foreigners; this would bring them to think
and act according to the Rules of Reason, by which a Spirit of
Industry, and Thrift, and Honesty, would be introduced among
them. And, indeed, considering how small a Tax would suffice for
such a Work, it is a publick Scandal that such a Thing should never
have been endeavoured, or, perhaps, so much as thought on.

To supply the Want of such a Law, several pious Persons, in many
Parts of this Kingdom, have been prevailed on, by the great
Endeavours and good Example set them by the Clergy, to erect
Charity-Schools in several Parishes, to which very often the richest
Parishioners contribute the least. In these Schools, Children are, or
ought to be, trained up to read and write, and cast Accompts; and
these Children should, if possible, be of honest Parents, gone to
Decay through Age, Sickness, or other unavoidable Calamity, by
the Hand of God; not the Brood of wicked Strolers; for it is by no
means reasonable, that the Charity of well-inclined People should
be applied to encourage the Lewdness of those profligate, aban-
doned Women, who croud our Streets with their borrowed or
spurious Issue.

In those Hospitals which have good Foundations and Rents to support them, whereof, to the Scandal of Christianity, there are very
few in this Kingdom; I say, in such Hospitals, the Children maintained, ought to be only of decayed Citizens, and Freemen, and be
bred up to good Trades. But in these small Parish Charity Schools
which have no Support, but the casual good Will of charitable
People, I do altogether disapprove the Custom of putting the
Children 'Prentice, except to the very meanest Trades; otherwise the
poor honest Citizen who is just able to bring up his Child, and pay
a small Sum of Money with him to a good Master, is wholly
defeated, and the Bastard Issue, perhaps, of some Beggar, preferred
before him. And hence we come to be so overstocked with 'Pren-
tices and Journeymen, more than our discouraged Country can
employ; and, I fear, the greatest Part of our Thieves, Pickpockets,
and other Vagabonds are of this Number.

Therefore, in order to make these Parish Charity Schools of great
and universal Use, I agree with the Opinion of many wise Persons,
that a new Turn should be given to this whole Matter.

I think there is no Complaint more just than what we find in almost
every Family, of the Folly and Ignorance, the Fraud and Knavery,
the Idleness and Viciousness, the wasteful squandering Temper of
Servants, who are, indeed, become one of the many publick
Grievances of the Kingdom; whereof, I believe, there are few Masters

that now hear me, who are not convinced by their own Experience. And I am very confident, that more Families, of all Degrees, have been ruined by the Corruptions of Servants, than by all other Causes put together. Neither is this to be wondered at, when we consider from what Nurseries so many of them are received into our Houses. The first is the Tribe of wicked Boys, where-with most Corners of this Town are pestered, who haunt publick Doors. These, having been born of Beggars, and bred to pilfer as soon as they can go or speak, as Years come on, are employed in the lowest Offices to get themselves Bread, are practised in all Manner of Villainy, and when they are grown up, if they are not entertained in a Gang of Thieves, are forced to seek for a Service. The other Nursery is the barbarous and desert Part of the Country, from whence such Lads come up hither to seek their Fortunes, who are bred up from the Dunghill in Idleness, Ignorance, Lying, and Thieving. From these two Nurseries, I say, a great Number of our Servants come to us, sufficient to corrupt all the rest. Thus, the whole Race of Servants in this Kingdom have gotten so ill a Reputation, that some Persons from *England*, come over hither into great Stations, are said to have absolutely refused admitting any Servant born among us into their Families. Neither can they be justly blamed; for, although it is not impossible to find an honest Native fit for a good Service, yet the Enquiry is too troublesome, and the Hazard too great for a Stranger to attempt.

If we consider the many Misfortunes that befal private Families, it will be found that Servants are the Causes and Instruments of them all: Are our Goods embezzled, wasted, and destroyed? Is our House burnt down to the Ground? It is by the Sloth, the Drunkenness or the Villainy of Servants. Are we robbed and murdered in our Beds? It is by Confederacy with our Servants. Are we engaged in Quarrels and Misunderstandings with our Neighbours? These were all begun and inflamed by the false, malicious Tongues of our Servants. Are the Secrets of our Family betrayed, and evil Repute spread of us? Our Servants were the Authors. Do false Accusers rise up against us? (an Evil too frequent in this Country) they have been tampering with our Servants. Do our Children discover Folly, Malice, Pride, Cruelty, Revenge, Undutifulness in their Words and Actions? Are they seduced to Lewdness or scandalous Marriages? It is all by our Servants. Nay, the very Mistakes, Follies, Blunders, and Absurdities of those in our Service, are able to ruffle and discompose the mildest Nature, and are often of such Consequence, as to put whole Families into Confusion.

Since therefore not only our domestick Peace and Quiet, and the

Welfare of our Children, but even the very Safety of our Lives, Reputations, and Fortunes have so great a Dependence upon the Choice of our Servants, I think it would well become the Wisdom of the Nation to make some Provision in so important an Affair: But, in the mean Time, and perhaps, to better Purpose, it were to be wished, that the Children of both Sexes, entertained in the Parish Charity-Schools, were bred up in such a Manner as would give them a teachable Disposition, and qualify them to learn whatever is required in any Sort of Service. For Instance, they should be taught to read and write, to know somewhat in casting Accompts, to understand the Principles of Religion, to practise Cleanliness, to get a Spirit of Honesty, Industry, and Thrift, and be severely punished for every Neglect in any of these Particulars. For, it is the Misfortune of Mankind, that if they are not used to be taught in their early Childhood, whereby to acquire what I call a teachable Disposition, they cannot, without great Difficulty, learn the easiest Thing in the Course of their Lives, but are always aukward and unhandy; their Minds, as well as Bodies, for want of early Practice, growing stiff and unmanageable, as we observe in the Sort of Gentlemen, who, kept from School by the Indulgence of their Parents but a few Years, are never able to recover the Time they have lost, and grow up in Ignorance and all Manner of Vice, whereof we have too many Examples all over the Nation. But to return to what I was saying: If these Charity-Children were trained up in the Manner I mentioned, and then bound Apprentices in the Families of Gentlemen and Citizens, (for which a late Law giveth great Encouragement)[3] being accustomed from their first Entrance to be always learning some useful Thing, they would learn in a Month more than another, without those Advantages can do in a Year; and, in the mean Time, be very useful in a Family, as far as their Age and Strength would allow. And when such Children come to Years of Discretion, they will probably be a useful Example to their Fellow Servants, at least they will prove a strong Check upon the rest; for, I suppose, every Body will allow, that one good, honest, diligent Servant in a House may prevent Abundance of Mischief in the Family.

These are the Reasons for which I urge this Matter so strongly, and I hope those who listen to me will consider them.

I shall now say something about that great Number of Poor, whc. under the Name of common Beggars, infest our Streets, and fill our Ears with their continual Cries, and craving Importunity. This I shall venture to call an unnecessary Evil, brought upon us for the gross

3 A law passed in 1715 by the Irish parliament to encourage wealthy families to apprentice charity children.

Neglect, and want of proper Management, in those whose Duty it is to prevent it: But, before I proceed farther, let me humbly presume to vindicate the Justice and Mercy of God and his Dealings with Mankind. Upon this Particular He hath not dealt so hardly with his Creatures as some would imagine, when they see so many miserable Objects ready to perish for Want: For it would infallibly be found, upon strict Enquiry, that there is hardly one in twenty of those miserable Objects who do not owe their present Poverty to their own Faults; to their present Sloth and Negligence; to their indiscreet Marriage without the least Prospect of supporting a Family, to their foolish Expensiveness, to their Drunkenness, and other Vices, by which they have squandered their Gettings, and contracted Diseases in their old Age. And, to speak freely, is it any Way reasonable or just, that those who have denied themselves many lawful Satisfactions and Conveniences of Life, from a Principle of Conscience, as well as Prudence, that they might not be a Burthen to the Public, should be charged with supporting Others, who have brought themselves to less than a Morsel of Bread by their Idleness, Extravagance, and Vice?[4] Yet such and no other, are for the greatest Number not only in those who beg in our Streets, but even of what we call poor decayed Housekeepers, whom we are apt to pity as real Objects of Charity, and distinguish them from common Beggars, although, in Truth, they both owe their Undoing to the same Causes; only the former is either too nicely bred to endure walking half naked in the Streets, or too proud to own their Wants. For the Artificer or other Tradesman, who pleadeth he is grown too old to work or look after Business, and therefore expecteth Assistance as a decayed Housekeeper; may we not ask him, why he did not take Care, in his Youth and Strength of Days, to make some Provision against old Age, when he saw so many Examples before him of People undone by their Idleness and vicious Extravagance? And to go a little higher; whence cometh it that so many Citizens and Shopkeepers, of the most creditable Trade, who once made a good Figure, go to Decay by their expensive Pride and Vanity, affecting to educate and dress their Children above their Abilities, or the State of Life they ought to expect?

However, since the best of us have too many Infirmities to answer for, we ought not to be severe upon those of others; and, therefore, if our Brother, thro' Grief, or Sickness, or other Incapacity, is not in a Condition to preserve his Being, we ought to support him to the best of our Power, without reflecting over seriously on the Causes that brought him to his Misery. But in order to this, and to turn our Charity into its proper Channel, we ought to consider who and

---

4 Swift's ruthless characterisation of the poor as agents rather than victims of poetry is the least edifying of his solemn reasoning. Women, servants and the poor are his favourite scapegoats.

where those Objects are, whom it is chiefly incumbent upon us to support.

By the antient Law of this Realm, still in Force, every Parish is obliged to maintain its own Poor, which although some may think to be not very equal, because many Parishes are very rich, and have few Poor among them, and others the contrary; yet, I think, may be justly defended: For, as to remote Country Parishes in the desart Parts of the Kingdom, the Necessaries of Life are there so cheap, that the infirm Poor may be provided for with little Burden to the Inhabitants. But in what I am going to say, I shall confine myself only to this City, where we are over-run, not only with our own Poor, but with a far greater Number from every Part of the Nation. Now, I say, this Evil of being encumbered with so many foreign Beggars, who have not the least Title to our Charity, and whom it is impossible for us to support, may be easily remedied, if the Government of this City, in Conjunction with the Clergy and Parish Officers, would think it worth their Care; and I am sure few Things deserve it better. For, if every Parish would take a List of those begging Poor which properly belong to it, and compel each of them to wear a Badge, marked and numbered, so as to be seen and known by all they meet, and confine them to beg within the Limits of their own Parish, severely punishing them when they offend, and driving out all Interlopers from other Parishes, we could then make a Computation of their Numbers;[5] and the Strolers from the Country being driven away, the Remainder would not be too many for the Charity of those who pass by, to maintain; neither would any Beggar, although confined to his own Parish, be hindered from receiving the Charity of the whole Town; because in this Case, those well-disposed Persons who walk the Streets, will give their Charity to such whom they think proper Objects, where-ever they meet them, provided they are found in their own Parishes, and wearing their Badges of Distinction. And, as to those Parishes which border upon the Skirts and Suburbs of the Town, where Country Strolers are used to harbour themselves, they must be forced to go back to their Homes, when they find no Body to relieve them, because they want that Mark which only gives them Licence to beg. Upon this Point, it were to be wished, that inferior Parish Officers had better Encouragement given them, to perform their Duty in driving away all Beggars who do not belong to the Parish, instead of conniving at them, as it is said they do for some

5 In 1724, Dublin councillors ordered parishes to regulate their mendicant poor by the distribution of badges. Swift was an enthusiastic, and obsessive, supporter of the compulsory scheme. As late as 1737, aged sixty-nine, he wrote and published *A Proposal for Giving Badges to Beggars*, for which see *Prose Works* XIII, pp. 129–140.

small Contribution; for the whole City would save much more by ridding themselves of many hundred Beggars, than they would lose by giving Parish Officers a reasonable Support.

It should seem a strange, unaccountable Thing, that those who have probably been reduced to Want by Riot, Lewdness, and Idleness, although they have Assurance enough to beg Alms publickly from all they meet, should yet be too proud to wear the Parish Badge, which would turn so much to their own Advantage, by ridding them of such great Numbers, who now intercept the greatest Part of what Belongeth to them: Yet, it is certain, that there are very many who publickly declare they will never wear those Badges, and many others who either hide or throw them away: But the Remedy for this, is very short, easy, and just, by tying them like Vagabonds and sturdy Beggars, and forcibly driving them out of the Town.

Therefore, as soon as this Expedient of wearing Badges shall be put in Practice, I do earnestly exhort all those who hear me, never to give their Alms to any publick Beggar who doth not fully comply with this Order; by which our Number of Poor will be so reduced, that it will be much easier to provide for the rest. Our Shop-Doors will be no longer crouded with so many Thieves and Pick-pockets, in Beggars Habits, nor our Streets so dangerous to those who are forced to walk in the Night.

Thus I have, with great Freedom delivered my Thoughts upon this Subject, which so nearly concerneth us. It is certainly a bad Scheme, to any Christian Country which God hath blessed with Fruitfulness, and where the People enjoy the just Rights and Privileges of Mankind, that there should be any Beggars at all. But, alas! among us, where the whole Nation itself is almost reduced to Beggary by the Disadvantages we lye under, and the Hardships we are forced to bear; the Laziness, Ignorance, Thoughtlessness, squandering Temper, slavish Nature, and uncleanly Manner of Living in the poor Popish Natives, together with the cruel Oppressions of their Landlords, who delight to see their Vassals in the Dust; I say, that in such a Nation, how can we otherwise expect than to be over-run with Objects of Misery and Want? Therefore, there can be no other Method to free this City from so intolerable a Grievance, than by endeavouring, as far as in us lies, that the Burden may be more equally divided, by contributing to maintain our own Poor, and forcing the Strolers and Vagabonds to return to their several Homes in the Country, there to smite the Conscience of those Oppressors, who first stripped them of all their Substance.

I might here, if the Time would permit, offer many Arguments to persuade to Works of Charity; but you hear them so often from the Pulpit, that I am willing to hope you may not now want them. Besides, my present Design was only to shew where your Alms would be best bestowed, to the Honour of God, your own Ease and Advantage, the Service of your Country, and the Benefit of the Poor. I desire you will all weigh and consider what I have spoken, and, according to your several Stations and Abilities, endeavour to put it in Practice; and God give you good Success, to whom, with the Son and Holy Ghost, be all Honour, &c.

The Grace of God, &c.

AN

EXAMINATION

OF

Certain Abuses, Corruptions, and Enormities,
in the City of Dublin.

Written in the Year 1732

This pamphlet was first published, anonymously, in Dublin in 1732, and quickly reprinted in London. Swift's talent for impersonation and his hatred of political jargon combine to produce a satirical caricature of Whig paranoia and its outrageous reasoning. Irish Whigs, in Swift's view, were usually grotesque versions of their English models. He felt so strongly about that 'cursed race of informers' that he once devoted an entire, passionate sermon to their corruption of society: see *False Witness*, in *Prose Works* IX, pp. 180–89.

AN

EXAMINATION

OF

Certain Abuses, Corruptions, and Enormities,
in the City of Dublin.

Written in the Year 1732

NOTHING is held more commendable in all great Cities, especially the Metropolis of a Kingdom, than what the *French* call the *Police*: By which Word is meant the Government thereof, to prevent the many Disorders occasioned by great Numbers of People and Carriages, especially through narrow Streets. In this Government our famous City of *Dublin*, is said to be very defective; and universally complained of. Many wholesome Laws have been enacted to correct those Abuses, but are ill executed; and many more are wanting; which I hope the united Wisdom of the Nation (whereof so many good Effects have already appeared this Session) will soon take into their profound Consideration.

As I have been always watchful over the Good of mine own Country; and particularly for that of our renowned City; where, (*absit invidia*)[1] I had the Honour to draw my first Breath; I cannot have a Minute's Ease or Patience to forbear enumerating some of the greatest Enormities, Abuses, and Corruptions spread almost through every Part of *Dublin*; and proposing such Remedies, as, I hope, the Legislature will approve of.

The narrow Compass to which I have confined my self in this Paper, will allow me only to touch the most important Defects; and such as I think, seem to require the most speedy Redress.

And first: Perhaps there was never known a wiser Institution than that of allowing certain Persons of both Sexes, in large and populous Cities, to cry through the Streets many Necessaries of Life: It would be endless to recount the Conveniences which our City enjoys by

---

1 No offence intended.

165

this useful Invention; and particularly Strangers, forced hither by Business, who reside here but a short time: For, these having usually but little Money, and being wholly ignorant of the Town, might, at an easy Price purchase a tolerable Dinner, if the several Criers would pronounce the Names of the Goods they have to sell, in any tolerable Language. And therefore until our Law-makers shall think it proper to interpose so far as to make those Traders pronounce their Words in such Terms, that a plain Christian Hearer may comprehend what is cryed; I would advise all new Comers to look out at their Garret Windows, and there see whether the Thing that is cryed be *Tripes*, or *Flummery*,[2] *Buttermilk*, or *Cowheels*. For, as Things are now managed, how is it possible for an honest Countryman, just arrived, to find out what is meant? For Instance, by the following Words, with which his Ears are constantly stunned twice a Day, *Muggs, Juggs, and Porringers, up in the Garret, and down in the Cellar*. I say, how is it possible for any Stranger to understand that this Jargon is meant as an Invitation to buy a Farthing's Worth of Milk for his Breakfast or Supper, unless his Curiosity draws him to the Window, or until his Landlady shall inform him? I produce this only as one Instance, among a Hundred much worse; I mean where the Words make a Sound wholly inarticulate, which give so much Disturbance, and so little Information.

The Affirmation solemnly made in the Cry of *Herrings*, is directly against all Truth and Probability; *Herrings alive, alive here*: The very Proverb will convince us of this; for what is more frequent in ordinary Speech, than to say of some Neighbour for whom the Passing-Bell rings, that *he is dead as a Herring*. And, pray how is it possible, that a *Herring*, which, as *Philosphers* observe, cannot live longer than One Minute, Three Seconds and a half out of Water, should bear a Voyage in open Boats from *Howth* to *Dublin*, be tossed into twenty Hands, and preserve its Life in Sieves for several Hours? Nay, we have Witnesses ready to produce, that many Thousands of these *Herrings*, so impudently asserted to be alive, have been a Day and a Night upon dry Land. But this is not the worst. What can we think of those impious Wretches, who dare in the Face of the Sun, vouch the very same Affirmative of their *Salmon*; and cry, *Salmon alive, alive*; whereas, if you call the Woman who cryes it, she is not ashamed to turn back her Mantle, and shew you this individual *Salmon* cut into a dozen Pieces. I have given good Advice to these infamous Disgracers of their Sex and Calling, without the least Appearance of Remorse; and fully against the Conviction of their own Consciences. I have mentioned this Grievance to several

2 Food made with wheatmeal or oatmeal, of Welsh origin.

of our Parish Ministers; but all in vain: So that it must continue until the Government shall think fit to interpose.

There is another *Cry*, which, from the strictest Observation I can make, appears to be very modern, and it is that of * *Sweet-hearts*; and is plainly intended for a Reflection upon the Female Sex; as if there were at present so great a Dearth of Lovers, that the Women instead of receiving Presents from Men, were now forced to offer Money, to purchase *Sweet-hearts*. Neither am I sure, that this *Cry* doth not glance at some Disaffection against the Government; insinuating, that while so many of our Troops are engaged in foreign Service; and such a great Number of our gallant Officers constantly reside in *England*; the Ladies are forced to take up with *Parsons* and *Attornies*: But this is a most unjust Reflection; as may soon be proved by any Person who frequents the *Castle*, our publick Walks, our Balls and Assemblies; where the Crowds of ** *Toupees* were never known to swarm as they do at present.

There is a *Cry* peculiar to this City, which I do not remember to have been used in *London*; or at least, not in the same Terms that it hath been practised by both Parties, during each of their Power; but, very unjustly by the *Tories*. While these were at the Helm, they grew daily more and more impatient to put all true *Whigs* and *Hanoverians* out of Employments. To effect which, they hired certain ordinary Fellows, with large Baskets on their Shoulders, to call aloud at every House, *Dirt to carry out*; giving that Denomination to our whole Party; as if they would signify, that the Kingdom could never be *cleansed*, until we were *swept* from the Earth like *Rubbish*. But, since that happy Turn of Times, when we were so *miraculously* preserved by just an *Inch*, from *Popery*, *Slavery*, *Massacre*, and the *Pretender*; I must own it Prudence in us, still to go on with the same *Cry*; which hath ever since been so effectually observed, that the true *political Dirt* is wholly removed, and thrown on its proper Dunghills, there to corrupt, and be no more heard of.

But, to proceed to other Enormities: Every Person who walks the Streets, must needs observe an immense Number of human Excrements at the Doors and Steps of waste Houses, and at the Sides of every dead Wall; for which the disaffected Party hath assigned a very false and malicious Cause. They would have it that these Heaps were laid there privately by *British Fundaments*, to make the World believe, that our *Irish* Vulgar do daily eat and drink; and, consequently, that the Clamour of Poverty among us, must be false; proceeding only from *Jacobites* and *Papists*. They would

---

* *A Sort of Sugar-Cakes in the Shape of Hearts.*
** *A new Name for a modern Periwig, and for its Owner; now in Fashion.*

confirm this, by pretending to observe, that a *British Anus* being more narrowly perforated than one of our own Country; and many of these Excrements, upon a strict View appearing Copple-crowned, with a Point like a Cone or Pyramid, are easily distinguished from the *Hibernian*, which lie much flatter, and with less Continuity. I communicated this Conjecture to an eminent Physician, who is well versed in such profound Speculations; and at my Request was pleased to make Trial with each of his Fingers, by thrusting them into the *Anus* of several Persons of both Nations; and professed he could find no such Difference between them as those ill-disposed People alledge. On the contrary, he assured me, that much the greater Number of narrow Cavities were of *Hibernian* Origin. This I only mention to shew how ready the *Jacobites* are to lay hold of any Handle to express their Malice against the Government. I had almost forgot to add, that my Friend the Physician could, by smelling each Finger, distinguish the *Hibernian* Excrement from the *British*; and was not above twice mistaken in an Hundred Experiments; upon which he intends very soon to publish a learned Dissertation.

There is a Diversion in this City, which usually begins among the *Butchers*; but is often continued by a Succession of other People, through many Streets. It is called the COSSING[3] *of a Dog*: And I may justly number it among our Corruptions. The Ceremony is thus: A strange Dog happens to pass through a Flesh-Market: Whereupon an expert *Butcher* immediately cries in a loud Voice, and the proper Tone, *Coss, Coss*, several Times: The same Word is repeated by the People. The Dog, who perfectly understands the Term of Art, and consequently the Danger he is in, immediately flies. The People, and even his own *Brother Animals* pursue: The Pursuit and Cry attend him perhaps half a Mile; he is well worried in his Flight; and sometimes hardly escapes. This, our Ill-wishers of the *Jacobite* Kind are pleased to call a *Persecution*; and affirm, that it always falls upon *Dogs* of the *Tory* Principle. But, we can well defend our selves, by justly alledging, that, when they were uppermost, they treated our *Dogs* full as inhumanly: As to my own Part, who have in former Times often attended these *Processions*; although I can very well distinguish between a *Whig* and a *Tory Dog*; yet I never carried my Resentments very far upon a *Party Principle*, except it were against certain malicious *Dogs*, who most discovered their Enmity against us in the *worst of Times*. And, I remember too well, that in the wicked Ministry of the Earl of *Oxford*;[4] a large Mastiff of our Party

3 A shout or cry over a great distance, of Indian origin.
4 Friend of Swift and leader of Tory party 1710–14. Defended and idealised by Swift, who always remained loyal to his memory.

being unmercifully *cossed*; ran, without Thinking, between my Legs, as I was coming up *Fishamble-street*; and, as I am of low Stature, with very short Legs, bore me riding backwards down the Hill, for above Two Hundred Yards: And, although I made use of his Tail for a Bridle, holding it fast with both my Hands, and clung my Legs as close to his Sides as I could; yet we both came down together into the Middle of the Kennel; where after rowling three or four Times over each other, I got up with much ado, amidst the Shouts and Huzza's of a Thousand malicious *Jacobites*: I cannot, indeed, but gratefully acknowledge, that for this and many other *Services* and *Sufferings*, I have been since more than over-paid.

This Adventure may, perhaps, have put me out of Love with the Diversion of *Cossing*; which I confess myself an Enemy too; unless we could always be sure of distinguishing *Tory Dogs*; whereof great Numbers have since been so prudent, as entirely to change their Principles; and are now justly esteemed the best *Worriers* of their former Friends.

I am assured, and partly know, that all the Chimney-Sweepers Boys, where Members of P——t chiefly lodge, are hired by *our Enemies* to sculk in the Tops of Chimneys, with their Heads no higher than will just permit them to look round; and at the usual Hours when Members are going to the House, if they see a Coach stand near the Lodging of any *loyal* Member; they call *Coach, Coach*, as loud as they can bawl, just at the Instant when the Footman begins to give the same Call. And this is chiefly done on those Days, when any Point of Importance is to be debated. This Practice may be of very dangerous Consequence. For, these Boys are all hired by Enemies to the Government: And thus, by the Absence of a few Members for a few Minutes, a Question may be carried against the *true Interest* of the Kingdom; and, very probably, not without an Eye towards the *Pretender*.

I have not observed the Wit and Fancy of this Town, so much employed in any one Article as that of contriving Variety of Signs to hang over Houses, where *Punch* is to be sold. The Bowl is represented full of *Punch*; the Ladle stands erect in the middle; supported sometimes by one, and sometimes by two Animals, whose Feet rest upon the Edge of the Bowl. These Animals are sometimes one black *Lion*, and sometimes a Couple; sometimes a single *Eagle*, and sometimes a spread One; and we often meet a *Crow*, a *Swan*, a *Bear*, or a *Cock*, in the same Posture.

Now, I cannot find how any of these Animals, either separate, or in Conjunction, are, properly speaking, fit Emblems or Embellishments, to advance the Sale of *Punch*. Besides, it is agreed among *Naturalists*, that no Brute can endure the Taste of strong Liquor; except where he hath been used to it from his Infancy: And, consequently, it is against all the Rules of *Hieroglyph*, to assign those Animals as Patrons, or Protectors of *Punch*. For, in that Case, we ought to suppose that the Host keeps always ready the real Bird, or Beast, whereof the Picture hangs over his Door, to entertain his Guests which, however, to my Knowledge, is not true in Fact: Not one of those Birds being a Proper Companion for a *Christian*, as to aiding and assisting in making the *Punch*. For, as they are drawn upon the Sign, they are much more likely to mute,[5] or shed their Feathers into the Liquor. Then, as to the *Bear*, he is too terrible, awkard, and slovenly a companion to converse with; neither are any of them all *handy* enough to fill Liquor to the Company: I do, therefore, vehemently suspect a *Plot* intended against the Government, by these Devices. For, although the *Spread-Eagle* be the Arms of *Germany*, upon which Account it may possibly be a lawful *Protestant* Sign; yet I, who am very suspicious of fair Out-sides, in a Matter which so nearly concerns our Welfare; cannot but call to Mind, that the *Pretender's* Wife is said to be of *German* Birth: And that many *Popish* Princes, in so vast an Extent of Land, are reported to excel both at making and drinking *Punch*. Besides, it is plain, that the *Spread Eagle* exhibits to us the perfect Figure of a *Cross*; which is a Badge of *Popery*. Then, as to the *Cock*, he is well known to represent the *French Nation*, our old and dangerous Enemy. *The Swan*, who must of Necessity cover the entire Bowl with his Wings, can be no other than the *Spaniard*; who endeavours to engross all the Treasures of the *Indies* to himself. The *Lion* is indeed the common Emblem of Royal Power, as well as the Arms of *England*: But to paint him black, is perfect *Jacobitism*; and a manifest Type of those who *blacken* the Actions of the best Princes. It is not easy to distinguish whether that other Fowl painted over the *Punch-Bowl*, be a *Crow* or *Raven*? It is true, they have both been held ominous Birds: But I rather take it to be the former; because it is the Disposition of a *Crow*, to pick out the Eyes of other Creatures; and often even of *Christians*, after they are dead; and is therefore drawn here, with a Design to put the *Jacobites* in Mind of their old Practice; first to lull us a-sleep, (which is an Emblem of Death) and then to blind our Eyes, that we may not see their dangerous Practices against the State.

To speak my private Opinion; the least offensive Picture in the whole Sett, seems to be the *Bear*; because he represents *Ursa Major*, or the *Great Bear*, who presides over the *North*; where the

5 To defecate.

Reformation first began; and which, next to *Britain*, (including *Scotland* and the *North of Ireland*) is the great Protector of the *true Protestant* Religion. But, however, in those Signs where I observe the *Bear* to be *chained*, I cannot help surmising a *Jacobite* Contrivance; by which, these Traytors hint an earnest Desire of using all *true Whigs*, as their Predecessors did the primitive Christians: I mean, to represent us as *Bears*, and then halloo their *Tory-Dogs* to bait us to Death.

Thus I have given a fair Account of what I dislike, in all the Signs set over those Houses that invite us to *Punch*. I own it was a Matter that did not need explaining; being so very obvious to common Understanding: Yet, I know not how it happens, but methinks there seems a fatal Blindness, to overspread our corporeal Eyes, as well as our intellectual; and I heartily wish, I may be found a false Prophet. For, these are not bare Suspicions, but manifest Demonstrations.

Therefore, away with these *Popish, Jacobite*, and idolatrous Gewgaws. And I heartily wish a Law were enacted, under severe Penalties, against drinking any *Punch* at all: For, nothing is easier, than to prove it a disaffected Liquor. The chief Ingredients, which are *Brandy, Oranges*, and *Lemons*, are all sent us from *Popish* Countries; and nothing remains of *Protestant* Growth, but *Sugar* and *Water*. For, as to Biscuit, which formerly was held a necessary Ingredient, and is truly *British*, we find it is entirely rejected.

But I will put the Truth of my Assertion past all Doubt: I mean, that this Liquor is by one important Innovation, grown of ill Example, and dangerous Consequence to the Publick. It is well known, that, by the true original Institution of making *Punch*, left us by Captain *Ratcliff*;[6] the Sharpness is only occasioned by the Juice of *Lemmons*; and so continued until after the happy *Revolution*. *Oranges*, alas! are a meer Innovation, and, in a manner, *but of Yesterday*. It was the Politicks of *Jacobites* to introduce them gradually: And, to what Intent? The Thing speaks it self. It was cunningly to shew their Virulence against his sacred Majesty King *William, of ever glorious and immortal Memory*. But of late (to shew how fast Disloyalty increaseth) they came from one to two, and then to three *Oranges*; nay, at present, we often find *Punch* made all with *Oranges*; and not one single *Lemon*. For, the *Jacobites*, before the Death of that immortal Prince, had, by a Superstition, formed a private Prayer; that, as they *squeezed* the Orange, so might that

6 Possibly Captain John Ratcliffe, (formerly John Sicklemore), who became Governor of Virginia in 1606. Punch was originally brought to England by sailors from India.

Protestant King be *squeezed* to Death: According to the known *Sorcery* described by *Virgil; Limus ut hic durescit, & haec ut cera liquescit*,[7] &c. And, thus the *Romans*, when they sacrificed an Ox, used this Kind of Prayer: *As I knock down this Ox, so may thou, O* Jupiter, *knock down our Enemies*.[8] In like Manner, after King *William's* Death, whenever a *Jacobite squeezed* an Orange, he had a mental Curse upon the *glorious Memory*; and a hearty Wish for Power to *squeeze* all his Majesty's Friends to Death, as he *squeezed* that Orange, which bore one of his Titles, as he was Prince of *Orange*. This I do affirm for Truth; many of that Faction having confessed it to me, under an *Oath of Secrecy*; which, however, I thought it my Duty not to keep, when I saw my dear Country in Danger. But, what better can be expected from an *impious* Set of Men, who never scruple to drink CONFUSION to all *true Protestants*, under the Name of *Whigs?* A most unchristian and inhuman Practice; *which, to our great Honour and Comfort, was* never *charged upon us, even by our most malicious Detractors.*

The Sign of two *Angels*, hovering in the Air, and with their Right Hands supporting a *Crown*, is met with in several Parts of this City; and hath often given me great Offence: For, whether by the Unskilfulness, or dangerous Principles of the Painters, (although I have good Reasons to suspect the latter) those *Angels* are usually drawn with such horrid, or indeed rather diabolical *Countenances*, that they give great Offence to every loyal Eye; and equal Cause of Triumph to the *Jacobites*; being a most infamous Reflection upon our able and excellent Ministry.

I now return to that great Enormity of City *Cries*; most of which we have borrowed from *London*. I shall consider them only in a *political* View, as they nearly affect the Peace and Safety of both Kingdoms: And having been originally contrived by wicked *Machiavels*, to bring in *Popery, Slavery*, and *arbitrary Power*, by defeating the *Protestant* Succession, and introducing the *Pretender*; ought, in Justice, to be here laid open to the World.

About two or three Months after the happy *Revolution*, all Persons who possess any Employment , or Office, in Church or State, were obliged by an Act of Parliament, to take the Oaths to King *William* and Queen *Mary*: And a great Number of disaffected Persons, refusing to take the said Oaths, from a pretended Scruple of Conscience, but really from a Spirit of *Popery* and Rebellion, they contrived a Plot, to make the swearing to those Princes odious in the Eyes of the People. To this End, they hired certain Women of ill

7 So that it may harden this clay, and melt this wax.
8 Livy, Bk. 1. In the original, a pig, not an ox, is sacrificed.

Fame, but loud shrill Voices, under Pretence of selling Fish, to go through the Streets, with Sieves on their Heads, and cry, *buy my Soul, buy my Soul*; plainly insinuating, that all those who swore to King *William*, were just ready to sell their *Souls* for an Employment. This Cry was revived at the Death of Queen *Anne*, and I hear still continues in *London*, with much Offence to all *true Protestants*; but, to our great Happiness, seems to be almost dropt in *Dublin*.

But, because I altogether contemn the Displeasure and Resentment of *High-flyers, Tories, and Jacobites*, whom I look upon to be *worse even than profest Papists*; I do here declare, that those Evils which I am going to mention, were all brought upon us in the * *worst of Times*, under the late Earl of *Oxford's* Administration, during the four last Years of Queen *Anne's* Reign. *That wicked Minister was universally known to be a Papist in his Heart. He was of a most avaricious Nature, and is said to have died worth four Millions, sterl. besides his vast Expences in Building, Statues, Plate, Jewels, and other costly Rarities. He was of a mean obscure Birth, from the very Dregs of the People; and so illiterate, that he could hardly read a Paper at the Council Table. I forbear to touch at his open, prophane, profligate Life; because I desire not to rake into the Ashes of the Dead; and therefore I shall observe this wise Maxim:* De mortuis nil nisi bonum.[9]

This flagitious Man, in order to compass his black Designs, employed certain wicked Instruments (which great Statesmen are never without) to adapt several *London* Cries, in such a Manner as would best answer his Ends. And, whereas it was upon good Grounds grievously suspected, that all *Places* at Court were sold to the highest Bidder: Certain Women were employed by his Emissaries, to carry *Fish* in Baskets on their Heads, and bawl through the Streets, *Buy my fresh Places*. I must, indeed, own that other Women used the same Cry, who were innocent of this wicked Design, and really sold their Fish of that Denomination, to get an honest Livelyhood: But the rest, who were in the *Secret*, although they carried *Fish* in their Sieves or Baskets, to save Appearances; yet they had likewise a certain Sign, somewhat resembling that of the *Free-Masons*, which the Purchasers of *Places* knew well enough, and were directed by the Women whither they were to resort, and make their Purchase. And, I remember very well, how oddly it lookt, when we observed many Gentlemen finely drest, about the Court-End of the Town,

---

* *A Cant-Word used by Whigs for the four last Years of Queen* Anne's *reign, during the Earl of* Oxford's *Ministry; whose Character here is an exact Reverse in every Particular.*

9 *Speak kindly of the dead.*

and as far as *York-Buildings*, where the Lord-Treasurer *Oxford* *dwelt*; calling the Women who cried *Buy my fresh Places*, and talking to them in the Corner of a Street, until they understood each other's Sign. But we never could observe that any Fish was bought.

Some Years before the Cries last mentioned; the Duke of *Savoy* was reported to have made certain Overtures to the Court of *England*, for admitting his eldest Son, by the Dutchess of *Orleans's* Daughter, to succeed to the Crown, as next Heir, upon the *Pretender's* being rejected; and that Son was immediately to turn *Protestant*. It was confidently reported, that great Numbers of People disaffected to the then *Illustrious* but now *Royal* House of *Hanover*, were in those Measures. Whereupon, another Sett of Women were hired by the *Jacobite* Leaders, to cry through the whole Town, *Buy my* Savoys, *dainty* Savoys, *curious* Savoys. But, I cannot directly charge the late Earl of *Oxford* with this *Conspiracy*, because he was not then chief Minister. However, this wicked Cry still continues in *London*, and was brought over hither; where it remains to this Day; and is in my humble Opinion, a very offensive Sound to every true Protestant, who is old enough to remember those *dangerous* Times.

During the Ministry of that corrupt and *Jacobite* Earl abovementioned, the secret pernicious Design of those in Power, was to sell *Flanders* to *France:* The Consequence of which, must have been the infallible Ruin of the *States-General*, and would have opened the Way for *France* to obtain that universal Monarchy, they have so long aimed at; to which the *British* Dominions must next, after *Holland*, have been compelled to submit. Whereby the *Protestant* Religion would be rooted out of the World.

A Design of this vast Importance, after long Consultation among the *Jacobite* Grandees, with the Earl of *Oxford* at their Head; was at last determined to be carried on by the same Method with the former: It was therefore again put in Practice; but the Conduct of it was chiefly left to chosen Men, whose Voices were louder and stronger than those of the other Sex. And upon this Occasion, was first instituted in *London*, that famous Cry of FLOUNDERS. But the Cryers were particularly directed to pronounce the Word *Flaunders*, and not *Flounders*. For, the Country which we now by Corruption call *Flanders*, is in its true Orthography spelt *Flaunders*, as may be obvious to all who read old *English* Books. I say, from hence begun that thundering Cry, which hath ever since stunned the Ears of all *London*, made so many Children fall into Fits, and Woman miscarry; *Come buy my fresh* Flaunders, *curious* Flaunders, *charming* Flaunders, *alive, alive, ho*; which last Words can with no Propriety of

Speech, be applied to Fish manifestly dead, (as I observed before in *Herrings* and *Salmon*) but very justly to ten Provinces, containing many Millions of living *Christians*. But the Application is still closer, when we consider that all the People were to be taken like *Fishes* in a Net; and, by Assistance of the *Pope*, who sets up to be the *universal Fisher of Men*, the whole innocent nation was, according to our common Expression, to be *laid as flat as a* Flounder.

I remember, my self, a particular Cryer of *Flounders* in *London*, who arrived at so much Fame for the Loudness of his Voice, as to have the Honour of being mentioned, upon that Account, in a Comedy. He hath disturbed me many a Morning, before he came within Fifty Doors of my Lodging: And although I were not, in those Days, so fully apprized of the Designs which our common Enemy had then in Agitation; yet, I know not how, by a secret Impulse, young as I was, I could not forbear conceiving a strong Dislike against the Fellow; and often said to my self, this Cry seems to be forged in the *Jesuites* School: *Alas, poor* England! *I am grievously mistaken, if there be not some* Popish *Plot at the Bottom.* I communicated my Thoughts to an intimate Friend, who reproached me with being too visionary in my Speculations. But it proved afterwards, that I conjectured right. And I have since reflected, that if the wicked Faction could have procured only a Thousand Men, of as strong Lungs as the Fellow I mentioned, none can tell how terrible the Consequences might have been, not only to these two Kingdoms, but over all *Europe*, by selling *Flanders* to *France*. And yet these Cries continue unpunished, both in *London* and *Dublin*; although, I confess, not with equal Vehemency or Loudness; because the Reason for contriving this desperate Plot, is, to our great Felicity, wholly ceased.

It is well known, that the Majority of the *British* House of Commons, in the last Years of Queen *Anne's* Reign, were in their hearts directly opposite to the Earl of *Oxford's* pernicious Measures; which put him under the Necessity of bribing them with Sallaries. Whereupon he had again Recourse to his old Politicks. And accordingly, his Emissaries were very busy in employing certain artful Women, of no good Life or Conversation, (as it was fully proved before Justice * *Peyton*) to cry that Vegetable commonly called *Sollary*, through the Town. These Women differed from the common Cryers of that Herb, by some private mark which I could never learn; but the Matter was notorious enough, and sufficiently talked of; and about the same Period was the Cry of *Sollary* brought over into this Kingdom. But since there is not, at this present, the least

---

* *A famous Whig Justice in those Times.*

Occasion to suspect the Loyalty of our Cryers upon that Article, I am content that it may still be tolerated.

I shall mention but one Cry more, which hath any Reference to Politicks; but is, indeed, of all others, the most insolent, as well as treasonable, under our present happy Establishment. I mean that of *Turnups*; not of *Turnips*, according to the best Orthography, but absolutely *Turnups*. Although this Cry be of an older Date than some of the preceding Enormities; for it began soon after the Revolution; yet was it never known to arrive at so great an Height, as during the Earl of *Oxford's* Power. Some People, (whom I take to be private Enemies) are indeed, as ready as my self to profess their Disapprobation of this Cry, on Pretence that it began by the Contrivance of certain old Procuresses, who kept Houses of ill Fame, where lewd Women met to draw young Men into Vice. And this they pretend to prove by some Words in the Cry; because, after the Cryer had bawled out *Turnups, ho, buy my dainty Turnups*, he would sometimes add the two following Verses.

> *Turn up the Mistress, and turn up the Maid,*
> *And turn up the Daughter, and be not afraid.*

This, say some political Sophists, plainly shews, that there can be nothing further meant in so infamous a Cry, than an Invitation to Lewdness; which, indeed, ought to be severely punished in all well regulated Governments; yet cannot be fairly interpreted as a Crime of State. But, I hope, we are not so weak and blind to be deluded at this Time of Day, with such poor Evasions. I could, if it were proper, demonstrate the very Time when those two Verses were composed, and name the Author, who was no other than the famous Mr. *Swan*, so well known for his Talent at Quibbling; and was as virulent a *Jacobite* as any in *England*. Neither could he deny the Fact, when he was taxed for it in my Presence, by Sir *Harry Dutton-Colt*, and Colonel *Davenport*, at the *Smyrna* Coffee-House, on the 10th of *June*, 1701,[10] Thus it appears to a Demonstration, that those Verses were only a Blind to conceal the most dangerous Designs of the Party; who from the first Years after the happy Revolution, used a Cant way of talking in their Clubs, after this Manner: *We hope to see the Cards shuffled once more, and another King* TURNUP *Trump:* And, *when shall we meet over a Dish of* TURNUPS? The same Term of Art was used in their Plots against the Government, and in their treasonable Letters writ in Cyphers, and decyphered by the famous Dr. *Wallis*,[11] as

---

10 I cannot trace the verses or the characters, but the Smyrna coffee-house was in Pall Mall, and a popular meeting-place for writers.

11 John Wallis (1616–1703). Renowned mathematician. Often employed by the Court to decode and decipher cryptic or suspect political messages.

you may read in the Tryals of those Times. This I thought fit to set forth at large, and in so clear a Light; because the *Scotch* and *French* Authors have given a very different Account of the Word TURNUP; but whether out of Ignorance or Partiality, I shall not decree; because, I am sure the Reader is convinced by my Discovery. It is to be observed, that this Cry was sung in a particular Manner, by Fellows in Disguise, to give Notice where those Traytors were to meet, in order to concert their villainous Designs.

I have no more to add upon this Article, than an humble Proposal, that those who cry this Root at present in our Streets of *Dublin*, may be compelled by the Justices of the Peace, to pronounce *Turnip*, and not *Turnup*; for, I am afraid, we have still too many Snakes in our Bosom; and it would be well if their Cellars were sometimes searched, when the Owners least expect it; for I am not out of Fear, that *latet anguis in Herba*.[12]

Thus, we are zealous in Matters of small Moment, while we neglect those of the highest Importance. I have already made it manifest, that all these Cries were contrived in the *worst of Times*, under the Ministry of that desperate Statesman, *Robert* late Earl of *Oxford*; and for that very Reason, ought to be rejected with Horror, as begun in the Reign of *Jacobites*, and may well be numbered among the Rags of *Popery* and *Treason:* Or if it be thought proper, that these Cries must continue, surely they ought to be only trusted in the Hands of *true Protestants* who have given Security to the Government.

---

12 A snake lurks in the grass. Virgilian proverb.

Appendix
Checklist of Swift's writings on Irish affairs

The following is a list of all Swift's prose-writings on Ireland. My principle of selection has been to include those texts, whether slight or substantial, well-known or neglected, typical or untypical, intended for publication or not, which show Swift's engagement with Irish affairs. As far as possible, the list reflects the chronological order of original composition, when such information is available. Because so many of Swift's pamphlets and tracts were published long after they were first written, I have included dates of their first printing, and the name and place of publication. After Swift's death, many individual items were published simultaneously in Dublin and London editions, often by the Dean's young cousin, Deane Swift, and the Dublin publisher, George Faulkner. Because Swift showed no interest in publishing his sermons, it is difficult, sometimes impossible, to know when they were first composed and preached. In placing them within a chronological order, I have followed the hints provided by Louis Landa in his 'Introduction to the Sermons', *Prose Works*, IX, pp. 133–37.

The Story of the Injured Lady, written in 1707, first published in 1746, by Faulkner in Dublin and Cooper in London. Swift's first pamphlet on Irish affairs. An allegorical complaint by Ireland about England's Act of Union with Scotland. Unpublished because Swift was courting those very Whigs who arranged the Union.

A Letter from a Member of the House of Commons in Ireland to a Member of the House of Commons in England, concerning the Sacramental Test, written in 1708, published in the same year by Morphew in London. Swift, in the disguise of an Irish M.P., warns a fictional London M.P. about the danger to Ireland of relaxing the Test Act which required dissenters to acknowledge the authority of the Established Church. A life-long obsession with Swift.

A Letter to a Member of Parliament in Ireland upon Choosing a New Speaker There, written in 1710, first published in 1765 by Hawkesworth in London and Faulkner in Dublin. Anonymous appeal to Irish Whigs to choose a Speaker who would ensure the preservation of the Test Act. Swift decided against publication because of political crises in London, one which led to him working for the Tories.

A Short Character of His Excellency Thomas, Earl of Wharton, Lord Lieutenant of Ireland, written in 1710 and printed, by Coryton, in London. Anonymous libel on former Lord Lieutenant for his support of Dissent. Written while writing for Tories on *Examiner*.

On Brotherly Love (Sermon), preached in December 1717, first published in 1754, by Faulkner in Dublin and Dodsley in London. One of the few sermons which can be accurately dated. An impassioned attack on friends of 'moderation' and Dissent.

On False Witness (Sermon), composed or preached during reign of George I, first published in 1762 by Faulkner. Devoted to the national evil of political informers.

A Proposal for the Universal Use of Irish Manufacture, written in 1720 and published by Waters in Dublin in same year. Swift's first pamphlet since appointment as Dean of St. Patrick's. Plea for economic self-reliance and boycott of English imports. Publication led to unsuccessful attempt by authorities to charge and convict author and printer of sedition.

A Defence of English Commodities, written in 1720, published in Dublin and London in same year. An ironic attack on his own *Proposal*, using the character of a fanatical English patriot.

The Wonderful Wonder of Wonders, and *The Wonder of all the Wonders*, written in 1720 and published the following year in London. Both pieces burlesque the madness of those who support the proposed Bank of Ireland, a topic mentioned by Swift at the end of his 1720 *Proposal*.

Subscribers to the Bank, written in 1721 and published by Harding in the same year. A mock-legal inventory of those gentry who hoped the bank would increase their wealth. This was the first time Swift employed John Harding, who would later publish *The Drapier's Letters*.

A Letter to the King at Arms, written in 1721 and published by Harding in the same year. An ironic protest by an impoverished gentleman who hopes for a financial miracle from the bank.

A Letter to a Young Gentleman, Lately enter'd into Holy Orders, written in 1720 and published in the same year in Dublin by Waters. Advice from a 'Person of Quality' on the need for a simple and humane style of preaching.

A Letter of Advice to a Young Poet, written in 1720, published the following year in Dublin by Hyde. On need for direct and unpretentious literary style in verse. Interesting proposals for encouragement of poetic excellence in Ireland.

A Letter from Dr. Swift to Mr. Pope, written in 1721, first published in 1741 by Faulkner in Dublin and Cooper in London. Epistolary essay reviewing his political, religious and literary career up to this point. Finally published, under Pope's supervision, as part of the correspondence between the two friends.

The Last Speech and Dying Words of Ebenezor Elliston, written in 1722, and published in Dublin in same year. A broadside 'confession' by a convicted criminal, defending the justice of his imminent execution.

Causes of the Wretched Condition of Ireland (Sermon), probably composed or preached after 1720, first published in 1762 by Faulkner. Indictment of absentee landlords and of English economic policy towards Ireland. Practical remedies recommended, useless speculation dismissed.

Some Arguments against Enlarging the Power of Bishops, written in 1723, published in the same year in Dublin by Hyde. A straight-faced, but anonymous, plea to defend the lower-clergy's historical right to tithes, an income now threatened by devaluation of gold and silver.

The Humble Representation of the Clergy of the City of Dublin, written in 1724, first published in 1765 by Deane Swift in London and Faulkner in Dublin. A 'collective' appeal by the Dublin clergy to their Archbishop, William King, to consider their economic distress.

A Letter to the Shopkeepers, Tradesmen, Farmers and Common-People of Ireland, written in 1724 and published by Harding in same year. The first of Swift's celebrated *Drapier's Letters.* Impersonating a tradesman of his own parish, Swift opens his campaign against William Wood, an English speculator granted a patent, without consultation in Ireland, to make and distribute copper coins for the Irish economy. Harding printed and cirulated two thousand copies.

A Letter to Mr. Harding the Printer, written in 1724 and published by Harding in same year. Written in response to newspaper-reports, (including some in Harding's own Dublin *Weekly-News Letter*), that a government committee had approved the patent. Drapier urges no compromise.

Some Observations upon a Paper, written in 1724 and published by Harding in same year. Addressed to the 'Nobility and Gentry of the Kingdom of Ireland', now the Drapier systematically dismisses the accuracy and legitimacy of the government Report. Advocates popular declarations of boycott.

A Letter to the Whole People of Ireland, written in 1724 and published by Harding in same year. Rhetorically, the most daring and notorious of the *Letters,* asserting Ireland's legislative independence from England. Lord Lieutenant Cartaret issues a legal proclamation against printer and author for certain passages 'seditious and scandalous'. Harding jailed.

Seasonable Advice to the Grand Jury, written in 1724 and printed without printer's name or place in same year. Anonymous leaflet urging members of the jury in the case against the printer and author to dismiss the charges. They did so, and were dismissed themselves. The Judge, Chief Justice Whitshed, was the same man who tried and failed to prosecute printer and author of Swift's 1720 *Proposal.*

An Extract etc., written in 1724, without name, place or date. A single sheet in which Swift quoted legal precedents from seventeenth-century cases showing the illegality of dismissing a grand-jury which refuses to comply with a judge's direction. Intended to embarrass Whitshed and uplift the jury.

A Letter to the Lord Chancellor Middleton, written in 1724, first published in 1735 by Faulkner in Dublin. Written during the proclamation against the Drapier, this letter was directed to the highest legal authority in Ireland. It defends the absolute and natural justice of the Drapier's arguments. Unusually, Swift wrote the pamphlet in his own name, though never admitting to being the Drapier. Suddenly realising the government's determination to prosecute, he decided not to publish. This pamphlet, though fifth in sequence, is usually referred to as the Sixth Letter.

A Letter to the Right Honourable the Lord Viscount Molesworth, written in 1724 and published by Harding in same year. Last of the *Letters* to be published during the campaign, this pamphlet sees Swift, posing again as the Drapier, addressing a well-known radical Whig noted for his liberal views on Irish legislative independence. It was the only issue on which Swift and Molesworth would have agreed. The Drapier, almost finished with Wood, now speaks of the importance of liberty for patriotic writers. Usually referred to as the Fifth Letter.

An Humble Address to Parliament, written in 1725, first published in 1735 by Faulkner in Dublin. The last of the *Letters*. An appeal to the Irish members to begin an economic revival by using some of the Drapier's practical proposals. Just as Swift was planning publication, word arrived that Wood's patent had finally been withdrawn, and the pamphlet was withheld.

An Account of Wood's Execution, written in 1725, first published in 1735 by Faulkner in Dublin. A short burlesque, alternating mock-solemn reportage with dramatic dialogue.

Doing Good (Sermon), composed and preached in late 1724 during pamphlet-campaign against Wood. First published in 1765 by Faulkner in Dublin and Hawkesworth in London. Swift uses his pulpit to defend and promote the Drapier, stressing the moral justice of resistance to the patent.

A Sermon upon the Martyrdom of King Charles I, preached on 30 January 1726, first published in 1765 by Faulkner in Dublin and Hawkesworth in London. This date was of great political significance to all churchmen, as it officially commemorated the murder of the lawful monarch. Swift makes the most of the occasion, mercilessly identifying all dissenters as regicides at heart and fanatics by nature. The kind of performance which confirms his reputation as extreme Tory.

A Short View of the State of Ireland, written in 1728 and published by Harding in the same year. An anonymous pamphlet printed by Sarah Harding, wife of the Drapier's printer, John, who had died in 1725. A bitter restatement of many of Swift's earlier complaints and proposals concerning the Irish economy.

An Answer to a Paper called a Memorial, written in 1728 and published by Harding in same year. As a famous pamphleteer, Swift was often sent other people's pamphlets for pre-publication consideration. This 'Answer' was to one of those schemes which suggested importing food to allay shortages. An impatient Swift here replies that graziers are the curse of a country which should be able to grow its own food, if it only had the freedom to do so.

The Intelligencer, printed by Harding in 1728. A small weekly paper begun in May 1728 by Swift and his friend Thomas Sheridan. Swift contributed seven articles or essays on topics literary, political and economic. No. 15 in the series was a reprint of his *Short View*, while No. 19 was a fictional letter from a 'Gentleman in the North of Ireland' to the Drapier on the disastrous economy and rising emigration.

A Letter to the Archbishop of Dublin concerning the Weavers, written in 1729, first published in 1765 by Deane Swift in London. An exasperated plea by Swift to the Archbishop to use his influence to promote economic and agricultural reforms. The first of many pamphlets in this year written for publication but then left aside.

Answer to Several Letters from Unknown Persons, written in 1729, first published in 1765 by Deane Swift in London. A weary review of the reasons for rising Protestant emigration from Ireland to the new colonies in America. Addressed to reformers like himself, Swift questions the very point of such appeals.

Answer to Several Letters from Unknown Hands, written in 1729, first published in 1765 by Deane Swift in London. Similar to previous pamphlet in its tired advocation of vital improvements needed for Irish economy. In addition, recommends the abolition of the Irish language and its culture in the interests of civilisation.

A Letter on Mr. Maculla's Project about Half-Pence, written in 1729, first published in 1759 by Faulkner in Dublin. James Maculla, a Dublin tradesman and pamphleteer, had offered Swift a proposal for minting Irish coins locally. Swift's reply is a serious and patient costing of the plan, but not an optimistic one.

A Modest Proposal, written in 1729, published by Harding in same year. Written while staying with friends in Markethill, Co. Armagh, this is the climax of Swift's frustration with reformers like himself, and one of the few pamphlets of this period he was determined to publish.

A Proposal that all the Ladies . . . should appear constantly in Irish Manufacture, written in 1729, first published in 1765 by Deane Swift in London and Faulkner in Dublin. A characteristically occasional pamphlet written in quick response to proposed legislation to increase taxes on wine, Swift's favourite drink. He argues that women's fashion is a more deserving target, and that wine is Ireland's only and necessary consolation. The bill was passed and the pamphlet set aside.

Maxims Controlled in Ireland, written in 1729, first published in 1765 by Deane Swift in London and Faulkner in Dublin. An unfinished manuscript-draft which argues that general theories about a nation's economic health are always contradicted, or 'controlled', by Ireland's unnatural condition.

The Substance of what was said by the Dean on receiving his Freedom, written in 1730, first published in 1765 by Deane Swift in London and Faulkner in Dublin. Written in the third-person, this is a short account by Swift himself of the public ceremony at which he received the freedom of the City of Dublin. He reviews his patriotic service to the nation, and acknowledges authorship of *The Drapier's Letters*.

A Vindication of his Excellency the Lord Cartaret, written in 1730 and published by Faulkner in Dublin in same year. Cartaret, a personal friend of Swift, had been attacked by Whigs for favouring Tories. Swift now gives an ironic apology, through an anonymous Dublin Whig, for Cartaret's political integrity, thereby exposing Whig philistinism.

An Answer to the Craftsman, written in 1731, first published in 1758 by Faulkner in Dublin. *The Craftsman*, a Tory paper, had revealed the presence of French recruiting officers in Ireland, an operation privately sanctioned by the Whig government. Here, in the disguise of a Whig official, Swift ironically defends such collusion, arguing that the ideal solution to Ireland's problems would be the exportation of the entire population.

On the Bill for the Clergy's Residing on their Livings, written in 1731, first published in 1789 by Dilly in London. An unfinished document drafted by Swift in response to proposed legislation, instigated by the Irish bishops, to increase their revenue while lessening that of the lower-clergy. An interesting partisan history of the protestant clergy in Ireland.

Considerations upon Two Bills . . . Relating to the Clergy of Ireland, written in 1732, first published by Moore in London in the same year. An amplified, but still anonymous, version of previous document. Swift attacks English place-men in the Irish hierarchy, and defends the right of the lower clergy to a just standard of living. Swift's influence in this debate was significant, and the bill was defeated.

A Proposal for an Act of Parliament to Pay Off the Debt of the Nation, written in 1732, published by Faulkner in Dublin in same year. Assuming the guise of a neutral English visitor, Swift suggests that the Irish national debt could be cleared immediately if the bishops surrender their wealth, a patriotic gesture he has no doubt they will perform.

An Examination of Certain Abuses, Corruptions, and Enormities in the City of Dublin, written and published in 1732 in Dublin. A satirical parody of Whig paranoia about Tory and Jacobite influence in everyday life in the city. Even the catch-cries of street vendors are interpreted as sinister codes for disloyalty. Interesting for Swift's attention to proverbs and slang.

The Humble Petition of the Footmen in and about the City of Dublin, written in 1732, first published in 1733 by Roberts in London and Faulkner in Dublin. A brief mock-petition to the Irish parliament to beware of traitorous Jacobites posing as ordinary footmen, thereby bringing the profession into disrepute.

The Advantages Proposed by Repealing the Sacramental Test, written in 1732 and published by Faulkner in Dublin in same year. More than twenty years since his first pamphlets on Dissent, Swift now returned to this obsessive issue. The Irish parliament was being urged by the new Lord Lieutenant, Dorset, to repeal the Test Act against dissenters. Here, and in the following pamphlets, Swift anonymously defends the Established Church against all such change.

Queries Relating to the Sacramental Test, written in 1732, published without an imprint in Dublin in same year. A short bulletin comprised of rhetorical questions about the possible outcome of toleration for dissenters.

The Presbyterians' Plea of Merit, written in 1733 and published by Faulkner in Dublin in same year. An 'historical' analysis of Dissent in England and Ireland, proving that it may never be trusted by the state.

Reasons Humbly Offered to the Parliament of Ireland for Repealing the Sacramental Test written in 1733, first published in 1738 by Davis in London. Here Swift employed the disguise of an Irish Catholic who argues that dissenters, once tolerated, should make common cause with their equally-oppressed Catholic brethren. (A fearful consequence Swift always used to justify the Act). But, as so often happened in controversies like this, the pamphlet was made redundant by the government's decision to withdraw the legislation. Yet again, it is tempting to see Swift's pamphlets having some significant bearing on the outcome.

Some Considerations in the Choice of a Recorder, written and published in 1733 in Dublin without imprint. An anonymous election-leaflet recommending, but not naming, a patriotic candidate for the office. Mr. Stannard M.P., Swift's preference, was duly elected Recorder.

Advice to the Free-Men of Dublin, written and published in 1733 in Dublin without imprint. Another electoral intervention by Swift. An anonymous broadside urging support for Humphrey French, Lord Mayor of Dublin, in the parliamentary elections for the city constituency. The government's candidate was defeated, and French won the seat.

Observations Occasion'd by Reading a Paper, Entitled 'The Case of the Woolen Manufacturers', written in 1733, first published in 1789 by Dilly in London. A reply to the traders' defence of importing foreign materials. Swift attacks them for disloyalty and mismanagement. Most unusually, he identifies himself as Dean of St. Patrick's.

Some Reasons Against the Bill for Settling the Tyth of Hemp, Flax etc. by a Modus, written in 1734, published in same year by Faulkner in Dublin. Swift writes here as spokesman for those clergy who opposed an imminent law which would lessen their income from tithes. Still obsessed with the material condition of his Church, he argues that wealthy absentee landlords, and not loyal clergy, should be penalised. The bill was shelved.

Letter on the Fishery, written in 1734, first published in 1749 by Grant in London. A short reply to a proposal published by the Scottish merchant, Francis Grant, that the fishing-industry should be encouraged. Although Swift was pleased to be asked for his views, and approved the scheme, he was sceptical about the proposal's fate in Ireland. Grant included Swift's personal reply in the text of a later pamphlet on the same issue.

Reasons Why we should not lower the Coins now current in this Kingdom, written in 1736, published in same year by Waters in Dublin. Text of a speech made by Swift, to an audience of Dublin merchants, to protest against a proposed devaluation of gold.

Concerning that Universal Hatred which prevails against the Clergy, written in 1736, first published in 1765 by Deane Swift in London and Faulkner in Dublin. A short, unfinished tract on State-robbery of the Church's wealth, mostly concerned with Henry VIII and the Reformation.

A Proposal for Giving Badges to Beggars, written in 1737 and published in same year by Faulkner in Dublin. Swift's last pamphlet on public affairs in Ireland, written when he was almost seventy, and openly signed by the Dean himself. An eccentric, but not untypical, scheme to regulate the movements of the poor, and to separate the 'deserving' from the 'criminal'.

The Last Will and Testament of Jonathan Swift, written in May 1740, first published in 1745 by Faulkner in Dublin. Written five years before his death, Swift's will is a most coherent and dignified document. Systematic and precise to the end, he leaves money aside for a mental asylum to be called St. Patrick's, and remembers every living friend with a gift or an endowment. Immediately after Swift's death, his will was published in short-form, then in its entirety, as a matter of public and literary interest. Thereafter, it was always included in editions of his works.

Select Bibliography

Most of the critical literature on Swift's pamphleteering career in Ireland comes in the form of articles and essays, but there are two major, and invaluable, exceptions. The only book-length study of the pamphlets is O. Ferguson's *Jonathan Swift and Ireland*, (Urbana, Illinois, 1962), an excellent, comprehensive account. The other is the third volume of Irvin Ehrenpreis's *Swift: The Man, His Works, and The Age*, i.e. *Dean Swift*, (London, 1983), a magisterial and eloquent narrative which gives a detailed biographical context to Swift's pamphleteering. Herbert Davis's edition of *The Drapier's Letters*, (Oxford, 1935; rev. bibliography 1965), has an exhaustive and scholarly introduction to these most celebrated of the Irish pamphlets. James Woolley's new edition of *The Intelligencer*, (Oxford, 1990), is a welcome contribution to Swift's Irish career.

Articles and Essays

BECKETT, J. C.	"Swift and the Anglo-Irish Tradition", *Focus: Swift*, ed. C. J. Rawson, London, 1971, pp. 155–170.
BERTELSEN, L.	"Ireland, Temple, and the Origins of the Drapier", *Papers in Language and Literature*, 13, 1977, pp. 413–419.
CARPENTER, A.	*The Irish Perspective of Jonathan Swift*, Wuppertaler Hochschulreden, 13, 1978, 20pp.
COLEBORNE, B.	"Jonathan Swift and the Literary World of Dublin", *Englisch Amerikanische Studien*, 10, 1988, pp. 6–28.
COUGHLIN, M.	" 'This Deluge of Brass': Rhetoric in the First and Fourth Drapier Letters", *Eire/Ireland*, 11, No. 2, Summer 1976, pp. 77–91.
DAVIES, G.	"A new edition of Swift's *The Story of the Injured Lady*", *Huntington Library Quarterly*, 8, August 1945, pp. 388–392.
DAVIES, G.	"Swift's *The Story of the Injured Lady*", *Huntington Library Quarterly*, 6, August 1943, pp. 473–489.
EHRENPREIS, I.	"Dr. S***t and the Hibernian Patriot", *Jonathan Swift 1667–1967 A Dublin Tercentenary Tribute*, ed. R. McHugh and P. Edwards, Dublin and London, 1967, pp. 24–37.

EWALD, W. B. Jr.   "M. B. Drapier", *Swift: Modern Judgements*, ed.
                          A. N. Jeffares, London, 1969, pp. 170–191.

GILBERT, J. G.   "The Drapier's Initials", *Notes and Queries*,
                          CCVIII, Vol. X, 1963, pp. 217–218.

GOODWIN, A.   "Wood's Halfpence", *English Historical Review*,
                          51, October 1936, pp. 647–674.

GUSKIN, P. J.   "Intentional Accidentals: Typography and Au-
                          dience in Swift's *Drapier's Letters*", *Eighteenth-
                          Century Life*, 6, n.s. 1, 1980, pp. 80–101.

KINKEAD—WEEKES, M.   "The Dean and the Drapier", *Swift Revisited*,
                          ed. D. Donoghue, Cork, 1968, pp. 41–55.

LANDA, L.   "*A Modest Proposal* and Populousness",
                          Modern Philology, 40, November, 1942, pp.
                          161–170.

LEIN, C.   "Jonathan Swift and the Population of Ireland",
                          Eighteenth Century Studies, 8, 1975, pp.
                          431–453.

MCMINN, J.   "Printing Swift", *Eire/Ireland*, 20, No. 1, 1985,
                          pp. 143–149.

MCMINN, J.   "A Weary Patriot: Swift and the Formation of
                          an Anglo-Irish Identity", *Eighteenth-Century
                          Ireland*, Vol. 2, 1987, pp. 103–113.

MACAREE, D.   "Reason and Passion Harmonised: *The
                          Drapier's Letters* and the Language of Political
                          Protest", *Canadian Journal of Irish Studies*, Vol.
                          2, No. 2, December 1976, pp. 47–60.

RAWSON, C. J.   "The Injured Lady and the Drapier: A Reading
                          of Swift's Irish Tracts", *Philological Society
                          Transactions*, 3, 1980, pp. 15–43.

ROSS, A.   "The Hibernian Patriot's Apprenticeship", *The
                          Art of Jonathan Swift*, ed. C. T. Probyn, Lon-
                          don and New York, 1978, pp. 83–107.

SCHMIDT, J.   "The Drapier's Letters", *Englisch Amerikanische
                          Studien*, 10, 1988, pp. 29–49.

SIMMS, J.   "Dean Swift and the Currency Problem", *Oc-
                          casional Papers of the Numismatic Society of
                          Ireland*, 20, 1978, pp. 8–18.

TREADWELL, J.   "Swift, William Wood, and the Factual Basis of
                          Satire", *Journal of British Studies*, 15, No. 2,
                          Spring 1976, pp. 76–91.

WITTOWSKY, G.   "Swift's *Modest Proposal*: the biography of an
                          early Georgian Pamphlet", *Journal of History
                          of Ideas*, 4, January 1943, pp. 74–104.

WOODRING, C.   "The Aims, Audience, and Structure of the
                          Drapier's Fourth Letter", *Modern Language
                          Quarterly*, XVIII, 1956, pp. 50–59.